FOLDING FIVE MINISTRIES
INTO
ONE POWERFUL
TEAM

Taking the Prophetic And Apostolic Reformation To The Next Powerful Level

BEN R. PETERS

Published by
KINGDOM SENDING CENTER
P. O. Box 25
Genoa, IL 60135

www.kingdomsendingcenter.org
ben.peters@kingdomsendingcenter.org
ISBN 0-9767685-2-6

Cover art by Robert Bartow ~ *www.bartowimages.com*
Cover and book design by *www.ChristianBookDesign.com*

CONTENTS

PREFACE

Many great books have been written by great Christian leaders in the past few decades on the subject of apostles and prophets and the reformation which has been taking place in the church because of the restoration of these two ministries. However the other three gift-ministries listed in Ephesians 4:11, which have been accepted for some time in the church, have received very little attention and focus in the body of Christ. And very little has been written about how these three can work together with the apostles and prophets.

One of our goals for this book is to convince the reader that when the apostles and prophets are empowered and released to their God-ordained function in the body of Christ, there will be a fresh resurgence of energy and passion in the evangelist, pastor and teacher. Each of these will find a freedom to focus and specialize on what God has called them to do. The results will be amazing. Without the valuable contributions of these other three ministries, the apostles and prophets will accomplish relatively little, but with all five functioning in unity, each doing what he does best, incredible results will manifest.

We also want to give the reader a glimpse into the church of the future—a church without cracks for people to fall through—a church which will mow down the enemy's ranks with vibrant power—a church that will be a very real demonstration and a very real presentation of the person of Jesus operating in His physical body on the earth.

We will draw from resources already available and add some concepts and insights that have not yet been taught to the church at large. Some of these may seem a bit radical or revolutionary, so be prepared, and keep your wineskin soft and pliable. We trust that you will find yourself enjoying the taste of new wine before you put down this book.

We will be frequently using the term "five-fold ministries." We understand that many prefer the term "ascension-gift ministries" and we respect that term as well. However, we don't feel that the difference is that significant to this particular study, so we will use the more widely-used term. Some also believe that the last two mentioned—pastor and teacher—should be considered as one combination gift, the pastor/teacher. They may be right, but I have not yet been convinced by their arguments. I also see a significant difference in the ministries and personalities of pastors and teachers. While most pastors do teach at some level, there are many teachers who do not have strong pastoral giftings.

Their focus is on knowledge and truth, while the pastors' focus is on loving the sheep and caring for their needs. They do, of course, work together to get the job done.

Disclaimer:

Before we get started in the subject of "folding five ministries into one powerful team," we want to clearly state the following disclaimer. All of us who are trying to teach others about the five-fold ministries are still a long way from the place where we can say we really understand everything about them.

These ministries are being restored, but I believe there is still so much more to learn. What we teach in this book will be adjusted many times in the years ahead. But we do feel that we can at least be successful in bringing God's purpose for these ministries into a sharper focus, as well as visualizing how they can work together for the benefit of the Kingdom of God.

Note:

1. For the sake of simplicity and readability, we may occasionally refer to any of the five-fold ministries with masculine pronouns. The writer by no means is implying that women cannot function in any of these ministries. We have seen many women endowed with these great gifts and encourage them to use them for the Kingdom of God.
2. Because we are attempting to redefine the term "pastor" to a more biblical meaning, we will be putting the term in quotes whenever we refer to it in the contemporary usage, that is, as the administrative leader of the local church.
3. Words, phrases or other portions of Scripture highlighted in various ways are the emphasis of this author, in order to draw attention to a specific point.
4. For a list of suggested reading about apostles and prophets, please go to the back of this book.

Chapter 1

THE VISION

Korea

In September, 2000, my wife, Brenda, and I were on our way to South Korea. We had come to know some very special Korean folk in the Chicago area, and they had opened the doors for us to visit several "on-fire" churches in South Korea. On the way, while crossing the North Pacific Ocean, I was praying for a special word for the nation we were about to visit for the first time.

My mind went back to the first day we had attended Pal Bok Presbyterian Church in the North Chicago suburb of Mount Vernon. We ministered in the English service in the morning and returned in the evening for their Sunday night prayer service. These folk, like many Korean Christians, spend much time praying together. While we were all praying, I felt a burden for the Christians of North Korea. I had recently heard about the terrible persecution of our brothers and sisters living under the terribly oppressive Communist regime.

While praying, I saw a very quick vision of the Korean Peninsula, and I saw large walls on the coast of North Korea begin to float away from the land. I knew God was saying that North Korea was going to open up. I shared the vision with the prayer warriors present, and our precious new Korean friends rejoiced with me, believing that God had spoken to us all.

Within two days the media was buzzing with the news that for the first time in almost a half-century, North and South Korea were going to begin talks. The two governments were going to allow a limited number of family members to cross the Demilitarized Zone, and get together with their relatives, after almost five decades of separation. In addition future discussions were being scheduled.

With this confirmation, I felt sure that I had heard from God. More confirmation would follow after arriving in South Korea. There we would see numerous clear signs that the nation was getting excited about the possibility of reunification with North Korea. Other western nations also began to restore relations and talks with the Communist North.

But now I was aware that we were just a few hours away from our first adventure into this divided peninsula, and I was asking the same God, who had shown me the vision in Illinois, to give me some divine wisdom to impact the church in South Korea. If God was truly going to open up the nation to the north, the church in the south needed to be prepared.

Some concepts began to stir in my mind and spirit. I felt then (and still feel today) that the key to being prepared for this coming golden opportunity was somehow directly related to the restoration of the five-fold ministries that are mentioned in Ephesians 4:11.

The first concept was that *there are still apostles and prophets*. The second is that *they need each other and God needs them to work together*. These two ministries are the foundation stones of the church, and foundation stones are always laid side by side. In reference to this, God had already been speaking to me about the changes in church structure that He was bringing to the church, even before reading Dr. C. Peter Wagner's excellent book, *Churchquake*.

God has always had apostles and prophets in the earth, even if they weren't given those particular titles. But most of them have carried on their ministries with a certain degree of independence. They have usually had a great enough anointing to attract both a following and enough finances to stay in the ministry. Unfortunately they often reacted with a negative attitude to those who disagreed with them. Many of them would separate themselves from each other because of spiritual pride and carry on with an attitude of "I don't care what anyone else thinks, I know I'm right."

These leaders, although used by God in many wonderful ways, did not understand the concept of the interdependence of apostles and prophets, partly because they had not really embraced these terms and identified with their true callings. They assumed that since God had spoken to them in a personal way numerous times before, then if He wanted to communicate something to them, He would talk to them directly. I personally heard a T. V. preacher express that attitude years ago, when someone tried to give him a word they felt was from God. He said, "God talks to me. If He wants to tell me something, He can tell me directly. I don't need someone else to tell me." The word from the other person may not have been from God, but the preacher was putting himself on dangerous ground, and revealed a point of pride in his life.

The truth is that God will not tell us everything He wants us to know directly. If we have a point of pride in that area and think that we are so spiritual that we don't need to listen to anyone else, then I believe that God will hold back His answer until we humble ourselves and listen to others that He has put in our life. This applies to leaders as well as the whole church.

God had revealed to me near the end of the year 2000, that He was restoring the original foundation of the church by bringing together apostles and prophets into strong working relationships. These leaders would become very **inter**dependent, rather than **in**dependent of one another. Apostles and prophets would work side by side and each would allow others to speak into his or her live.

This highlighted the important truth, already mentioned above, that **apostles and prophets need each other. Even more importantly, God needs and is requiring them to work together.** His Kingdom agenda demands that these two important ministries team up and blend their giftings, so that God's strategy for bringing in the harvest will be implemented on planet earth. The great and exciting news is that God is doing exactly what He was saying to me. In unprecedented ways, apostles and prophets are joining forces and listening to each other to confirm what God is speaking to them.

Men like Dr. C. Peter Wagner and Dr. Bill Hamon have made very similar statements and are applying their convictions in very practical ways. Dr. Wagner, in *Apostles and Prophets,* writes an entire chapter entitled, *"Hitching Apostles to Prophets."*[1] He goes on to declare in the contents page that, *"Apostles can do certain good things on their own. Prophets can do certain good things on their own. But hitched together, they can change the world!"*

Having been reminded by the Holy Spirit that apostles and prophets were coming together, I knew that God wanted to draw the apostles and prophets of South Korea together for the purpose of preparing South Korean churches and Christians for the day when North Korea would finally open its doors to the gospel. **I knew that if we could bring these leaders into a time of seeking God together in humility, they would clearly hear from God and develop a strategy to bring a powerful and united presentation of the gospel to the North.**

Then God began to give me a picture of how all of the five-fold ministry gifts would be involved. We will give much greater detail in the chapters to come, but let me share now what I believe is the primary function of each of the five-fold ministries.

Simple Definitions

A. **Apostles:** These are God's generals who have spent time with their commander-in-chief and know His ways. They began as disciples who followed, served and learned from their Master. Then they became apostles, or "sent forth ones." They have been sent from their place of learning from Him, to their place of service for Him, where they will implement His divine plans. They are, in short, *the chief administrators of the Kingdom of Heaven on the earth.* They will usually have other strong giftings in one of the other four ministries, and bring those giftings with them in their service as apostles. Thus they may be prophetic apostles, teaching apostles, etc.

B. **Prophets:** These are like advisors to the apostles and other ministries. Their primary function is to listen to God's voice and get day-to-day or moment-by-moment updates from the throne room. The information they receive is then passed on to the apostolic leaders who are in charge of administrating the Kingdom of Heaven on the earth or to whomever they are instructed to speak.

C. **Evangelists:** Apostles and prophets may know how the battle should go, and lead the charge on the battlefield, but it is the army of evangelists that will infiltrate the territory of the enemy and bring home the trophies of war. Many of these evangelists may be young and somewhat inexperienced, but they will be led by those with greater maturity. They will use many different gifts and talents to attract and convert the lost. Some will be prophetic evangelists, others will do signs and wonders. Still others will use music and drama to draw the unbeliever. They will be placed in balanced teams through the revelatory gifts of the prophets and the administrative skills of the apostles.

D. **Pastors:**When the evangelists return with their trophies of war, they bring them into the sheepfold where they are immediately cared for by those who have the gift of pastoring. They are given love and assurance that they will be cared for and protected. They are given healing from their war wounds inflicted on them by their previous commanders. They are introduced by these pastors to the wonderful benefits of being cared for by the Great Shepherd of their souls. Under the care of these "under-shepherds," they grow in spiritual strength and maturity.

E. **Teachers:**Working side by side with the pastors are the teachers. They share with the converts and with the whole church, the exciting truths that God is revealing. They help to equip the young Christians with the knowledge of the Word of God that will give them strength for the battles that they will certainly be a part of. Some teachers will focus on basic principles of life and doctrine, while others will specialize in very specific subjects.

The Strategy

As I meditated on that long flight over the North Pacific, the picture was becoming clear. If the apostles and prophets of South Korea gathered together and seriously sought the Lord with open hearts and minds, God would give them the master strategy for reaching North Korea. Then they would begin to prepare evangelistic teams from all of the churches that would cooperate.

There would be prophetic evangelists, healing evangelists and miracle-working evangelists. There would be worship evangelists and those who would use drama and the arts to convey the message of hope and love. They would be under the prayer covering and supervision of the apostles and prophets, who would put these teams together, combining people from different churches, and target them for certain cities and regions. Many apostles and prophets would also accompany these teams and provide ongoing leadership for them.

Finances would be raised in advance to send the teams and to provide food and other gifts to the impoverished North Korean people. They would reveal to the North Koreans that their God cares about every need in their lives. The thrust would be a united, non-denominational demonstration of God's love.

Following the teams of evangelists would be teams of pastors and teachers, who would nurture and teach the spiritual babes and cause them to grow in strength and love. The purpose would be first to protect the lambs from the wolves, and second, make them strong so that they would also become soldiers in the army of God, serving according to the gifts of God in their life.

The pastors who would follow the evangelists would not necessarily be what we call "pastors" in our present church establishment. But rather, they are those who have the gift and calling of nurturing and loving the needy. They will serve under the apostles and prophets who cover them as spiritual fathers. They will fill the role that their giftings qualify them for, rather that what church tradition calls for.

Sharing the Vision

When we arrived in Seoul, South Korea, and began to minister through our faithful interpreters, we began to share this vision with leaders we met. In the conferences that had been planned for us, we were privileged to minister to more than one hundred senior "pastors" and many other church leaders. We were not sure of how much these folks understood or accepted our teaching, but we believed we had been called to share this vision.

The following year, we were back again in South Korea. Again we shared the vision for North Korea. And once again we had the privilege of ministering to scores of "pastors" and leaders and discovered that they were gathering on a regular basis from a variety of churches, many from cities several hours away. They came with an awareness that they were part of an apostolic reformation and that the five-fold ministries were being restored. This opened up the opportunity to share more of the fresh concepts that God had been giving me in regards to the five-fold ministry. Many of these will be shared in this book. With the language and culture barrier, we as Westerners don't always know what an Easterner is thinking or embracing, but we believe that God had a reason for us to share this information with our dear friends in South Korea, and that the message will have an eternal impact on the future of both North and South Korea.

More recently, as we will share, we have been challenged to share this basic concept and apply it in North American cities where God has given us favor with church leaders. We have only just begun to move into this arena, but it is one of the most exciting challenges that God has ever called us to work on.

Chicago

Before our second trip to Korea, and just a month or so before the 9/11 disaster, we were headed for a brief three-week incursion into the Chicago area. The 1800 mile trip from Spokane in our 33 foot motor home gave me a lot of time to meditate, especially when the rest of the family was sleeping.

Coming off a busy time spent with family (including five young grandchildren) in Eastern Washington, I hadn't had a lot of time to really seek God for a specific message for the Chicagoland area. I began to ask God to speak to me with some special nugget of truth or revelation. What God gave me was actually a series of four visions during the trip. For me, a vision is a quick visual impression on the screen of my mind. Each vision, after the first one, built on the previous one, and left me with a great excitement for what God would do for us there.

First Vision—The Unconnected Group

The first thing I saw was a group of individuals standing within an unmarked circle. It was obvious that they were part of the same group of people, but each one had a significant amount of space between them and the others. Each one seemed to have something in their hands, which were held behind their backs. I understood that these were the gifts that God had given them for the church.

Then I saw a big hand, which I knew was the hand of God. It came behind one of the individuals on the outside of the circle, and gave him a big push towards the middle and towards the others in the group. The force of God's hand was so strong that the man took several steps forward and right up to someone before he could stop himself.

I perceived that God was doing this to all the members of the group. The interpretation of this vision has been ongoing, but the basic point is this.

Christians in the body of Jesus all have been given gifts to bless the others in the body, but because of fear, pride, jealousy, or other issues of the flesh, they were not willing to use their gifts for the body.

The main reason they held back their gifts was fear, both of looking foolish and of exposure. All of them knew that they had faults that would make them targets for criticism, if people found out too much about them. The interesting thing was that the gifts that they held back were designed to help the others to overcome their faults and weaknesses. In other words, God will use your gifts to solve my problems, and my gifts to solve yours or someone else's in the group.

Both Paul and Peter revealed this truth in their epistles. Paul wrote to Timothy to stir up the gift that God had given him through the laying on of his hands. He followed this up with the exhortation, *"For God did not give us the spirit of fear, but of power, and of love and of a sound mind."* (II Timothy 1:6, 7) Very few Christians know that this famous verse follows the exhortation to stir up or rekindle the flame of the spiritual gifts that God has given Timothy.

Obviously Timothy had a problem with timidity when it came to using his gifts for the Kingdom of God. Paul called it a spirit of fear. In verse 8, he exhorts Timothy not to be ashamed or fearful to partake in the sufferings of Christ with him. The implication is that using your gifts can get you into trouble. Certainly, Paul had proven that in his eventful ministry. His list of troubles and trials fill a significant amount of space in some of his epistles.

Peter wrote, *"As each one has received a gift, so minister it to one another as good stewards of the manifold grace of God."* (I Peter 4:10).

After making it clear that each one has been given at least one gift, Peter instructs us to be good stewards of God's grace by serving one another with the Holy Spirit's gifts. The clear and direct implication is that if we don't serve one another with these gifts, we are not being good stewards of God's grace.

God's grace is an incredibly valuable commodity, and God has entrusted it to us to distribute to others. We do that by using our gifts. Through these gifts the Holy Spirit can reveal, heal and deliver from anything the enemy has thrown at us. But God has ordained that we should remain interdependent on one another rather than being independent of each other. If we don't minister our gifts to each other, we will all have problems we can't solve, because **God's answer to many of our problems will come through the gifts he has given to someone else**.

Sometime after the 9/11 disaster, I was reminded of the above vision and realized that God had used this event to push people together. America and the world found reasons to come together and the church of Jesus Christ, with its many different factions, also came together in many wonderful ways. It was probably just a very partial fulfillment to what the vision meant, but it gave me hope that the fulfillment of the second vision may not be too far away.

Second Vision—The Football Huddle

After meditating for some time on the meaning of the first vision, God gave me another. This time I saw the same group of people in a football huddle. They were each offering their abilities and gifts to the team and planning the next play, which the coach had sent in from the sidelines. As I meditated on the meaning of this vision, I began to clearly see the five-fold ministry in operation. There are eleven positions on an American football team, but I saw five separate functions on the team.

The Football Field

First, let's understand the playing field. The field represents the two spiritual kingdoms. At one end is the Kingdom of God. At the other end is the kingdom of Satan. One is light and the other is darkness. The line of scrimmage represents the line of battle between the two forces. Behind the line of scrimmage is all the territory and possessions of the Kingdom of God. Ahead of us is the territory controlled by Satan.

God's five-fold ministry team is on the offense. The goal is to move the ball forward so that we can move the line of scrimmage deeper into the enemy's territory. To do so, we have to move the ball across the enemy lines, where we take the risk of being tackled and hurt. But it is the only way that we can possess the territory that he has previously held. That territory holds precious souls, who are held as slaves to sin and suffering.

The Center

The center is the first player to touch the ball, which to me, represents God's word to us, including the gospel and its power. The center represents the prophet, who is a central ministry in the church. In my book entitled, *The Dynamics of Biblical Prophetic Ministry,* I shared the results of my research on the frequency of mention of all of the five-fold ministries. The references to prophecy and the prophet were three times the total of all the other four combined. Prophets and their ministry (both the true and the false) are almost everywhere you look in Scripture.

The reason for the centrality of the prophetic ministry, in my opinion, is that God is, and always has been, a communicating God. He created man for fellowship, and fellowship requires communication. The prophet and his ministry help facilitate that continuous communication between God and man. The prophet, like the center, who transfers the ball to the quarterback, transfers the word of the Lord to the administrator of the ministry team, the apostle.

The Quarterback

The apostle is like the quarterback of the team. He has spent the most time with the coach, learning how the coach thinks, and going over the fine details of every play. The rest of the players know what they, themselves, are supposed to do, but the quarterback knows what each of the players must accomplish, in order to make the play successful. The quarterback has the respect of the other players and they all listen to him for specific instructions before they engage the other team. Even so the apostle is respected by the other ministry team members, and they look to him to administrate the Holy Spirit's strategy to run a successful spiritual play and to defeat the other team, coached by our adversary, the devil.

Guards and Tackles

On either side of the center are guards and tackles. They are protectors who help push back the enemy and also prevent the other team from encroaching on their previously gained territory. These are the pastors and teachers, who through their ministry of loving encouragement and impartation of divine knowledge, provide protection to those who have been freed from the enemy's clutches. They also support and protect the other ministries, who are trying to advance the Kingdom of God, and gain more ground against the enemy.

The guards would represent the pastors, who are called to guard and protect the sheep under their care. The tackles would be the teachers, who are always ready to tackle anyone who tries to sneak behind their lines like wolves in sheep's clothing, teaching things that will destroy the body of Jesus. Teachers know that the truth is the most powerful defense against the deceptions of the enemy.

Ball Carriers and Receivers

That leaves us with the ball carriers and receivers. These are the various types of evangelists, whose passion is to take the gospel across the line into the enemy's territory. Like those who gain ground on the football field, they want to move the yardsticks forward to enlarge the possessions of the Kingdom of God.

When souls are brought from darkness to the Light of the World, the line of scrimmage moves forward a little. When the church is not fulfilling its call and falls asleep at its post, the enemy can push us backward and make gains for his kingdom. He does this through many devices, including the stealing of our children and our communities, putting them on his side, thus moving the yardsticks in his favor.

The evangelists love adventure and are not afraid of danger. As soon as the enemy identifies who is carrying the ball, that person becomes the immediate target of every man on the enemy's team. Each one will be trying to bring him down with a bruising tackle. In spite of this fact, these courageous warriors will enthusiastically carry the ball every chance they get, and they will penetrate the enemy's defenses as far as they can. When the evangelists are successful in making forward progress (even though they get severely bruised up in the process), the rest of the team moves quickly forward to possess the territory that now belongs to them. They quickly establish a new base of operations (their new line of scrimmage) and try to move forward again from there.

For every center and every quarterback, there are usually five ball carriers and receivers, and two guards and two tackles. This, to me, is a pretty good model for the distribution of the five-fold ministry. We should have many more evangelists than any other ministry. Unfortunately, our present church structure is not conducive to the training or empowering of evangelists. Part of the problem is that when churches are run by pastors, instead of apostles, the concern is mostly for the needs of the sheep who are already in the fold, because they still need so much care. But apostles see the bigger picture and can impress upon the church the need for raising up evangelists.

There are many potential evangelists that just need a little encouragement, training and some financial support. The apostles and prophets should be giving vision and passion to these untapped evangelists and sending them out into the enemy's camp. The pastors and teachers should be ready to deal with those they bring to them, those who have been redeemed from the tyranny of the enemy. The apostles and prophets should be much involved in preparing the pastors and teachers for their tasks as well.

Just as every member of a football team must give his best to fulfill his individual assignment, as determined by the coach and administrated by the quarterback, so should every member of the fivefold ministry function as God has ordained, under the administrative leadership of His chosen apostles. So many ministries have self-destructed because of a missing team member, or a lack of submission to God's chosen administrator by some member of the team.

Third Vision—The Heavenly Huddle

The third vision was also a great encouragement. Directly above the huddle on the football field, I saw a huddle in the Heavenlies. The angels were planning their strategy to correspond to what we would be doing on the field. I was aware that because we had come together and united our forces for one common cause, the angels were able to really work on our behalf. I was reminded of the promises made by Jesus in Matthew 16, and 18, that declare that whatever we bind or loose on earth would be bound or loosed in heaven. **True unity in the Spirit enables us to activate the angelic forces to accomplish in the heavenly realm what we are dealing with in the natural realm.**

Another way to explain it is that we deal with people in the visible realm, while angels are fighting with satanic powers in the invisible realm. Paul declared that *"we wrestle not against flesh and blood, but against principalities and powers, against the rulers of darkness*

of this world, against spiritual wickedness in high places." (Ephesians 6:12).
This is where prophetic intercession is so valuable. Just as prophetic
people from time to time give significant words to apostles, they also,
like the football center, stand strong against the enemy in spiritual
intercession, so that the divine play will be successful.

Fourth Vision—The Canopy

The final vision in this series was of a white and glorious covering
over the football field. It was a beautiful glory dome. I understood
this to be the blessing of the presence of God. A domed stadium also
provides protection from the unpredictable elements. It provides a
controlled environment. Because God had brought the team together
and released his five-fold ministry team against the enemy, He had
also released His angelic forces on His and our behalf. The result
was that the enemy had to flee and give up his control of the power
of the air. It gave our side a distinct and overwhelming advantage,
like the early church had in the Book of Acts, because the enemy
could not use his power of deceit and subtle cunning.

This vision made it very clear that we should not have to work so
hard to win the war against unbelief in the hearts of non-Christians.
When we let God humble us and cooperate by humbling ourselves
and submitting to His divine plans (including accepting His five-
fold ministries), His glory comes down and gives us an awesome
advantage over the power of Satan. Instead of the difficult struggle to
win one soul, people begin to cry out, "What must I do to be saved?"
Like the early church, we should frequently see thousands saved at
a time, and many people should be added to the church daily.

GOD'S HOUSE

Paul clearly declares that the church is built on the foundation of
the apostles and prophets (Ephesians 2:20). While some may cling

to the theory that apostles and prophets are not for today, I'd like to point out that their biblical support for that theory is extremely fragile. I have dealt with this issue in some detail in previous books, including *"Signs and Wonders, To Seek or Not To Seek."* In seminary, I did an extensive exegesis from the Greek text of Ephesians 4:11-16. My study found that the text clearly indicates that all five ministry gifts were given by Jesus, and would be needed until the church, the body of Jesus, is completely united in faith and maturity. We will not go into detail in this book, but rather we will proceed with the hope that the reader accepts the present day existence of all five gift-ministries.

The Foundation—Apostles and Prophets

Scripture has established that the foundation is composed of the apostles and prophets, with Jesus Christ being the Chief Corner Stone. (Ephesians 2:20). For some time, I wondered if I could fit the other ministries into the divine building, or temple of God. The answer kept evading me until I finally found the missing ingredients. I had missed some of the most important parts of the building.

Let me give you my present understanding of how the five-fold ministries represent different parts of the temple of God. As I mentioned earlier, God has been bringing apostles and prophets into a functional unity and laying them side by side to give a strong foundation to the twenty-first century church.

First of all, we can make the obvious observation that the foundation is the first part of the building to be built. If we try to build the walls without a foundation, the building has no future. It will certainly self-destruct. Even so, we can and will see that the other ministries are released into their destinies only when the apostles and prophets are first released to function as such.

The foundation stones must also be strong and willing to carry the weight of all the problems in the church. While the walls may hold up the roof, the foundation carries the weight of every part of the house. These stones are laid in the ground, partly visible and partly hidden. Apostles and prophets must be grounded in a solid, but private and personal relationship with God, and they will not always be understood by others. The fact is, however, that they will have a powerful impact on the rest of the building. **They establish the shape of the structure, and their strength will determine how large the building can grow.**

God has equipped the apostles and prophets to handle the pressure, if and when they work together. Without the prophets the apostles will become rigid and not flexible enough to adapt to a growing building. Without apostles, the prophets will not have the structural strength to carry any weight and the building will topple. But together they supplement each other's weaknesses with their strengths, and together they can perform their responsibilities as foundation stones in the house.

Today we are transitioning from the concept that the pastors are the foundation stones of the church. These precious servants of God were given to the church for a specific function in the body of Jesus. They were never meant to bear the weight of the whole building. They were given to be lovers and protectors of the sheep. They were not called to be administrators of large portions of the Kingdom of God on the earth. But we will get into that a little later.

Pastors—The Visible Structure

One of the key responsibilities of the pastor is to protect and shelter the sheep. We build walls and roofs on the foundations to provide protection from the elements, wild animals and evil people. Inside the house, between the walls and under the roof, the atmosphere is controlled. We stay warm in the frigid winter and cool in the hot summer. We sleep in peace and comfort and have cupboards and pantries full of food and necessities, as well as a few luxuries. When we are sick, we are nourished and cared for. When we come home injured at work or on the battlefield, we are nursed back to health.

Pastors are called to see that every person in the house is safe and warm and well fed. They make sure there are plenty of resources available and those who are sick or injured are cared for with compassion and skill. They are like doctors, nurses, nutritionists and psychologists. They care about the spiritual and physical health of each one, and they provide conditions for continual spiritual growth.

Teachers — The Windows

Teachers are the ones who focus on understanding the Word of God. Without windows letting the light in, the house is in darkness. The teachers bring illumination to the church so that we are not in darkness and easily deceived. Paul emphasizes the importance of this ministry in Ephesians 4:14. It declares that the five-fold ministries were given so that we would not be like children, tossed to and fro by every wind of doctrine. Although all ministries contribute to this maturity, it is the function of the teacher in particular to protect us from false doctrine.

We also depend on teachers to reveal the depth of the riches of the promises of God. When the light is dim, we can't read the fine print, but when the light is bright, the details come alive. This is the joy and passion of the teacher. He wants us to know how great our God is and how rich His Word is with promises for us.

When teachers are free and empowered to study and discover fresh and exciting truths and share them with the church, there is a continual excitement in the church. People love to hear the nuggets of truth that teachers dig out of the Scriptures. It feeds their soul and satisfies their longing for a greater understanding of the spiritual realm.

Teachers and pastors should work together like apostles and prophets do. Although pastors are often expected to feed the sheep, pastors (the Greek word is the word for shepherd) really just lead the sheep to the food. Pastors may also be teachers, but their primary function is not to teach, but to lead the sheep to the teachers. Teachers are not usually equipped to be loving, compassionate caretakers of the sheep. They go ahead and scout out the best pastures to bring the sheep to and report to the shepherd. Both pastors and teachers should know their specialties and use each other to supplement their weaknesses.

Evangelists—The Doors

The apostles and prophets are concerned with the building of the Kingdom of God and are willing to lay down their lives as foundation stones to support it. The pastors and teachers focus on the health and prosperity of the sheep that God has put in the house of God. But the evangelist is concerned with one main thing. He wants to bring more sheep into the safety of the fold. He is represented by the door of the house, which he is always opening to let in another sheep he has brought to the safety of the sheepfold. He may work mostly one-on-one, or he may speak to huge crowds, but his goal and passion is always to rescue souls from the kingdom of darkness and bring them into the Kingdom of God.

The evangelist will develop and utilize his gifts to reveal the power and love of God and to persuade and convince people to come to Jesus. He may use the power of reason and logic and historical evidences to reach the university crowd. Or he may focus on signs and wonders and miracles to attract the hungry masses, who just want some visible evidence or assurance that there is a God who loves them and can help them in their need.

But invariably, the evangelist will be opening the door of the house and bringing another little lamb or a large number of them. They then become the responsibility of the pastor and teacher, under the supervision of the apostles and prophets, who will also influence their growth and destiny.

Chapter 2

THE FIVE-FOLD MINISTRY IN THE OLD TESTAMENT

A lthough the five-fold ministry is clearly a New Testament concept, we can certainly see some prophetic pictures and types in the Old Testament of the various five-fold ministries.

THE LAST DAYS PROPHECIES

There are two virtually identical prophecies that foreshadow all five New Testament ministry gifts. These prophecies are recorded in Isaiah 2:2, 3, and in Micah 4:1, 2. These prophecies would be referred to as millennium prophecies by many Bible scholars, but I personally believe that most prophecies that speak to natural Israel have a corresponding spiritual interpretation to spiritual Israel, which is the church.

The passages begin with, *"Now it shall come to pass in the latter days."* We are clearly in the last days of the church age and I want to show you a prophetic picture of what God will restore to the church in these last days.

The next statement is, *"the mountain of the Lord's house shall be established on the top of the mountains, and be exalted above the hills; and all nations shall flow to it."* This can be interpreted that God will place his glory on the church and that that glory will be easily seen by people far and wide. The mountain speaks of glory and strength. Thus, the glory and strength of the Lord's house will be established on top of the glory and strength of the other things, which appear to be high and mighty, and His house will be exalted above them.

We are also told that all nations will flow to the "mountain of the Lord's house." We do believe that multitudes from every nation will flow to the house of God in these last days. Indeed, we have surely begun to see it happening in many nations in recent years at an accelerating pace.

Now let us go on and see how God will do what He wants to do through people who have been given His gifts.

1. The Evangelist

Isaiah 2:3 begins with the statement, *"Many people shall come and say, 'Come and let us go up to the mountain of the Lord, to the house of the God of Jacob.'"* This is the function of the evangelist. He wants to bring people to meet Jesus. Notice that it says that *many* people would come to others and say, "Hey guys, let's go mountain climbing; let's go see what's happening up there. Everyone is talking about it. Jesus is doing all kinds of miracles for people again up there on the mountain. Come on let's go!"

Again, I would like to make it clear that I believe that there should be more evangelists than any other of the five-fold ministries. These evangelists may be prophetic evangelists, worship evangelists, healing and miracle evangelists, or they may use any other approach, including the arts, but they will always be finding some way to bring people up to the mountain to meet with Jesus.

2. The Teacher

The evangelist goes on to talk about the ministry of Jesus on the mountain. We do believe that in the millennium Jesus will be physically present in Jerusalem, but before that, in the sunset of this church age, Jesus will work through his anointed leaders. The next statement made by the evangelist is this: *"He will teach us His ways."* He is teaching us His ways through the ministry of His anointed teachers.

God has been raising up many anointed teachers in the past few decades that have revealed some wonderful, life-changing truths. Without their input, the church would not have entered into many of the spiritual possessions we now enjoy.

3. The Pastor

The next statement made is *"And we will walk in His paths."* It is the pastor, or shepherd, that leads us by still waters, and in paths of righteousness (Psalm 23:2, 3). Through today's shepherds, Jesus leads His sheep to the pleasant pastures and the still waters. There they are nourished and strengthened, while under the protective watch of their loving shepherds.

It should be made clear, at this point, that there are not two different words in the Hebrew or Greek, as we have in English. We call a shepherd of people, a pastor, but in the original languages there was only one word. I know that in other languages as well, such as Spanish and Korean, there is only one word for both the shepherd of sheep and the shepherd of people. The word in Spanish happens to be "el pastor," which is used for both kinds of shepherds.

4. The Apostle

We are next informed that, *"Out of Zion will go forth the law."* This, of course refers to the apostle, who is in charge of the government of the church. The apostle brings order and structure and discipline when it is needed. Zion is the city of God. The apostles have been in Zion with God, but are sent forth by Him, when He knows they are ready to represent Him properly. They go forth, bringing divine justice as they administrate the Kingdom of God on the earth.

5. The Prophet

The final statement is, *"And the word of the Lord from Jerusalem."* The word of the Lord comes to us primarily through the prophet. Of course, our main source for the word of God comes from the Bible, the written word. But the Bible is a totally prophetic book and most of the Bible was written by people known as prophets. God continues to speak His fresh "Rhema" words through His present-day prophets. God is a communicating God and will never limit Himself to what He has spoken in the past. None of us have the right to gag the mouth of God.

APOSTLES AND PROPHETS

The term "Apostle" is not found in most of our English translations of the Old Testament, but Old Testament kings and other leaders, such as judges, are a very clear type of the New Testament apostle. Their basic function was administrating God's Kingdom on the earth. I believe that this is the most concise job description of the apostle. The apostle is God's representative on the earth. He is charged with stewardship of God's earthly Kingdom. The Kings of Israel, who walked with God, understood that same responsibility. Notice the request of Solomon, when God asked him what he wanted from Him.

"And Your servant is in the midst of Your people whom You have chosen, a great people, too numerous to be numbered or counted.

Therefore give to Your servant an understanding heart to judge
Your people, that I may discern between good and evil. For who is
able to judge this great people of Yours?" (1 Kings 3:8,9)

Twice Solomon called himself "Your servant," and three times
he referred to Israel as "Your People." Solomon knew that he was a
steward of God's people, and that he needed God's wisdom to rule
them. This is the precise attitude and perspective of an apostle. He
considers himself to be the ultimate servant with a very important
stewardship responsibility. His people are not "his" people, they
are God's.

King David clearly functioned apostolically. He began with a
strong prophetic anointing, and was called a prophet by Peter in Acts
2:30, but when he was functioning as the king of Israel he accepted
a powerful apostolic role.

Apostles and Prophets Need Each Other

The biblical legacy left to us concerning the record of the Kings
of Israel and Judah give us rich insights into the role of apostles and
prophets. As we have already pointed out, God intended apostles
and prophets to be co-workers and to be interdependent on one
another in a very special way.

We mentioned above that David was called a prophet, yet he was
functioning as an apostle. We need to understand that although our
gifts and callings are never recalled, we can transition from one role to
another. At some levels, or in some situations, our roles may change
quite frequently. When starting a new church and Christian school at
the same time, I was changing roles continuously. I have functioned
in a great many roles, while being prepared for my present ministry.
The same thing holds true for my very gifted and dedicated wife.
Today, our ministry is more focused, but we can still fulfill roles that
are not our specialties, when we need to.

The most important point I wish to make here is that every king had prophets who brought the word of the Lord to them. David, who was called a prophet, still had several other key prophets who spoke to him the word of the Lord. He could have had the attitude, "I'm a prophet myself, so why do I need any other prophets around, telling me what to do?" But David knew that while He was functioning as a king, with an apostolic mantel, he needed prophets, who were focusing on hearing the voice of God.

Apostles, as stated earlier, are those who have been with Jesus (Mark 3:14, Acts 4:13). They know His ways. This was especially true of men like David and Moses. But they are not allowed to just linger forever in that wonderful place of intimacy, like Mary sitting at the feet of Jesus. Rather, Jesus sends them out to represent Him and administrate His Kingdom for him.

Apostles do not have the luxury of hours and hours alone with God, while they are on assignment. They must tend to the harvest field and supervise and organize the workers. They must see that the Master's storehouses and granaries are filled with the bounty that He deserves. Certainly, apostles, like ambassadors, return home and spend time with their Master in the throne room for times of renewal and updates from the throne, but their calling is on the field, serving and working long hours on behalf of the Kingdom of God.

That is where the prophet comes in. Most often, the prophet will not be a great administrator. And while he is in the role of the prophet, God does not want him to be busy with practical details. His function is to be one who always has his ears open to God. He spends much time seeking God for revelation and for pure words for the church, for the world and for needy individuals. While the apostle is busy administrating God's Kingdom, the prophet is listening to hear what God might have to say to the apostle or evangelist or pastor or teacher.

In modern government, we find a parallel in the relationship of our president or prime minister, with his or her entourage of advisers, who are specialists in various fields. The president or prime minister is the one responsible for the decisions, which must be made, but he has others who are listening and gathering information from their various sources. He would never have time to personally gather all that information and still do his job of administration. And if the advisers had to administrate, they could never find the time to research the information needed to administrate wisely.

Likewise, we discover that the kings in the Bible had a variety of prophets who spoke into their lives. In my personal research I discovered that **every king of any significance has at least one reference to prophets involved with his reign in the biblical record.** I will mention some of these now. References are omitted for the sake of readability. You will find their stories in the books of I and II Kings and I and II Chronicles, as well as in the introduction to the books of many of the major and minor prophets.

Kings Matched With Prophets

1. King Saul was anointed and later rebuked by the prophet, Samuel.
2. David was anointed by Samuel and also had Nathan, Gad and Zadok, the priest, who was also called a seer.
3. Solomon had Nathan, Zadok and Zabud, Nathan's son.
4. King Reheboam had Shemiah.
5. Abijah had Iddo.
6. Jereboam had Ahijah as well as a "Man of God from Judah," who prophesied to him.
7. King Asa had Azariah, Oded, and Hanani.
8. Baasha had Jehu, the son of Hanani.
9. Ahab, one of the most evil kings of Israel, had numerous interactions with prophets. Ahab first had Elijah, then an unnamed prophet, then an unnamed "man of God," then "certain men of the sons of the prophets" and then Micaiah.

Of course, he also had 400 false prophets of Baal.

10. Good king Jehoshophat had Jehaziel and Elieazer.

11. Ahaziah had Elijah.

12. Jehoram of Judah received a letter from Elijah.

13. Jehoram of Israel had Elisha.

14. Jehu, Jehoahaz, and Jehoash also had Elisha.

15. Athaliah and Joash had Jehoiada the prophetic priest.

16. Joash also had Zechariah, the son of Jehoiadah and other "prophets."

Lest you grow weary of reading this list, I will stop here. I think my point is clear by now. Kings, both small and great, wicked and righteous, were given prophetic counselors to help them make wise decisions, and to warn some of them not to continue leading the nation into depravity. Even so, apostles today need prophetic input to make their decisions prudently.

Restoration Leaders Encouraged Through Prophets

When Cyrus the Persian decreed that the Jews could return to their homeland, God raised up leaders, such as Ezra the Priest, Zerubbabel, the first governor and Nehemiah, the king's cupbearer and the later governor of the region. In the books written by Ezra and Nehemiah we read about the impact of the prophets among them. We also find similar information in the books of the restoration prophets, which are the last four books of the Old Testament.

Ezra, Zerubabbel and Jeshua, who oversaw the restoration of the temple, and Nehemiah, who restored the city walls, all functioned in apostolic roles, which can easily be seen with a little reading of books mentioned above. But without the prophets encouraging them, they would not have been successful.

Notice these power-packed verses:

*"Then the prophet Haggai and Zechariah the son of Iddo,
prophets, prophesied to the Jews who were in Judah and Jerusalem, in the name of the God of Israel, who was over them. So
Zerubbabel the son of Shealtiel and Jeshua the son of Jozadak rose
up and began to build the house of God which is in Jerusalem;
and the prophets of God were with them, helping them."*
(Ezra 5:1, 2)

*"So the elders of the Jews built, **and they prospered through the
prophesying of Haggai the prophet and Zechariah the son of
Iddo**. And they built and finished it, according to the command-
ment of the God of Israel, and according to the command of Cyrus,
Darius, and Artaxerxes king of Persia. (Ezra 6:14)*

Notice the underlined word "so" in the first passage. First the
prophets prophesied. The result was the completion of the project. It
is interesting to note as well that the prophets stayed with the project
and helped the leaders. We don't know if they helped with the physical labor, or if they continued to speak words of encouragement to
the workers and leaders, but my hunch is that they also put their
hands to the work to get it completed faster, while speaking words
of encouragement to those around them.

Application of the Apostle/Prophet Relationship

Often we find application of this principle in other relationships,
such as marriage. When the husband is functioning in an administrative role, often the wife will be the prophetic voice. His inclination
may be to reject her advice, because he has more factual information
about the situation than she does. But she may be in a prophetic
mode, where she is at rest and listening to God, while he is busy
administrating. She may be sensing something that has nothing to
do with the available empirical information on the issue.

Other times the wife will be busy with a project and her husband will become the prophetic advisor. It is important that we keep our ears open to the prophetic people that God has put in our midst, especially when we are busy doing things for the Kingdom of God. It is also important to recognize what mode we are in at the time.

OLD TESTAMENT PASTORS AND TEACHERS

Pastors

The terms "Pastor" and "Shepherd" (both of which use the same Hebrew word) are used 70 times in the Old Testament. Some of them refer to natural shepherds of sheep, but a significant number of them refer to men who have the responsibility of leading God's people. For example, Moses asked God to set another man over the congregation, so that the people would not be like sheep without a shepherd (Numbers 27:16, 17).

Others refer to God as a shepherd of men. The most famous is of course Psalm 23. We are often reminded that God cares for us as a shepherd cares for his sheep. The twenty-third Psalm gives us a clear job-description of a good shepherd or pastor.

The shepherd makes sure his sheep are not in want. He supplies their basic needs. The shepherd takes them to the green pastures and clear, still waters, and leads them on paths of righteousness, or justice. He restores the hurting sheep. He stays with them and comforts them so that they are not afraid, even when walking through the dark shadows. He blesses them and anoints their head with oil and keeps them close to him all the days of their lives.

The true shepherd has a very deep commitment to his sheep, and he will never leave them or forsake them. As the prophet Zechariah declared, *"Woe to the worthless shepherd, who leaves the flock! A sword shall be against his arm and against his right eye; his arm shall completely wither, and his right eye shall be totally blinded."* (Zechariah 11:17).

It is interesting that leaders like Moses, Joshua and David were referred to as shepherds. In some Scriptures we don't know who exactly is being referred to when pastors or shepherds are being addressed and often verbally chastised, as occurs frequently in the prophets. It seems that there were certain people thought of as pastors among the people. They seem to be distinct from prophets and priests.

For example in Jeremiah 2:8, we seem to have four categories of leaders rebuked for their behavior. They are: 1. Priests; 2. Those who teach the law, (possibly the Levites or Scribes); 3. Pastors; 4. Prophets. The Hebrew word used in this verse for pastor is ra-ah, the normal word for shepherd, but the New King James Version, and several others translate it "ruler" and some commentaries also suggest that it refers to civic rulers.

My personal guess is that the term shepherds in this Scripture, and many others, is referring to the elders of the city. They functioned like civic rulers, and sat in the gates of the city. Sitting in the gates indicated the fact that they were protectors of the city, like shepherds in the door of the fold. The parallel goes to the New Testament, where Paul instructed the elders of Ephesus,

"Take heed to yourselves and all the flock, among whom the Holy Spirit has made you overseers, to shepherd the church of God which He purchased with His own blood. For I know this, that after my departure savage wolves will come in among you, not sparing the flock." (Acts 20:28, 29)

Similarily, Peter told all elders who would read his epistle,

"Shepherd the flock of God which is among you, serving as overseers, not by constraint but willingly, not for dishonest gain but eagerly." (I Peter 5:2)

Clearly there were certain people in the Old Testament referred to as pastors or shepherds; whether kings, like David, or rulers, like

Moses and Joshua, or elders of the city who watched over the people of their city. They were the forerunners of the New Testament pastors.

Teachers

Teachers are also referred to occasionally in the Old Testament, but not as often as pastors or shepherds. In fact there are only seven times the word teacher is used in both the singular and plural. It is clear however that there were people known as teachers. David declared,

"I have more understanding than all my teachers, for Your testimonies are my meditation." (Psalm 119:99)

Although the term "teacher" is not used much in the Old Testament, the verb form "teach" is used 104 times. It is often used as a command, such as,

"You shall teach them diligently to your children, and shall talk of them when you sit in your house, when you walk by the way, when you lie down, and when you rise up." (Deuteronomy 6:7)

Here and in many other places, the parent is the teacher. In many other passages, people ask God to teach them what they need to know. David prays,

"Show me Your ways, O Lord, teach me your paths." (Psalm 25:4)

As we referred to in our discussion on pastors, Jeremiah referred to "those who teach the law" (Jeremiah 2:8). These could be the Levites or the Scribes, who in the New Testament, were those who read and copied the Scriptures. At any rate there were certainly people who were known as teachers, thus preparing the way for the New Testament ministry of teacher.

OLD TESTAMENT EVANGELISTS

There are several references to the ministry of the evangelist in the Old Testament, but the term itself is not used. The meaning of the word, "evangelist," is one who brings good news, which is also translated the gospel. The word "gospel," of course, is used to describe the good news of salvation through the death and resurrection of Jesus. Thus "gospel" is not an Old Testament term.

But the ministry of the evangelist is clearly exampled in the Old Testament. One of the most famous verses is found in Isaiah 52:7.

"How beautiful upon the mountains are the feet of him who brings **good news**, *who proclaims peace, who brings glad tidings of good things, who proclaims salvation, who says to Zion, 'Your God reigns'."*

Another excellent passage is the following:

"Oh Zion, You who bring **good tidings**, *get up into the high mountain; O Jerusalem, you who bring* **good tidings**, *lift up your voice with strength, lift it up, be not afraid; Say unto the cities of Judah, 'Behold your God!'" (Isaiah 40:9)*

Clearly these passages speak of those who were commissioned to be messengers to the people. There was good news to tell the people according to the prophets who were looking into the future.

Four Evangelists of the Old Testament

My personal favorite example of Old Testament evangelists is found in the book of II Kings. Four unnamed lepers demonstrated the pure principles of evangelism, which can be for us a wonderful model to emulate.

These four lepers were starving outside the city of Samaria.

Surrounding the city was the army of the Assyrians. Inside the city, people had run out of food and were starving. The king of Israel blamed the prophet and threatened to take his life. Knowing what the king was planning, Elisha prophesied that the very next day, there would be so much food that it would become extremely inexpensive.

The four lepers decided to see if the Assyrians would have any pity on them. They knew they would die if they didn't. What they didn't know was that God had created a noise to make the Assyrian army think that many armies were coming to attack them. They had fled, leaving everything they possessed behind. The four lepers found their camp full not only of food, but of jewels, clothing, horses and donkeys, etc.

The lepers began to haul off the loot to hide it somewhere, and return for more. Suddenly, a deep truth hit them.

*"Then they said to one another, 'We are not doing what is right. This day is a day of **good news**, and we remain silent. If we wait until morning light, some punishment will come upon us. Now therefore, come, let us go and tell the king's household.' " (II Kings 7:9)*

Several powerful principles can be noted.

1. These men had defects. Lepers were not society's upper class.
2. They had no training in soul winning, but they saved a whole city.
3. They were aware that they had good news, and it was not right to keep it to themselves.
4. They decided to go to the king's household rather than to other lepers. Thus they were able to bring the good news to everyone quickly.

We don't have to be perfect before we can tell others about the good news that we have discovered. We just need to have good news that will help the other person. Many people hesitate to witness because they have defects and feel like others won't accept the message because of the messenger.

Many times we are afraid to witness to the upper classes of society, but the lepers went right to the top. Leaders are looking for answers as much as the lower classes of society, and they can respond to the good news faster and more efficiently than non-leaders once they accept it themselves.

We have clearly seen that the five-fold ministry is plainly foreshadowed and exampled in the Old Testament. Some of it is prophetic and some was part of the fabric of Old Testament life. Most of the ministries which are needed in the body of Christ are found in the five ministries we have been talking about. And now let us move forward into the New Testament and see how these ministries functioned in the early church.

Chapter 3

THE FIVE-FOLD MINISTRY
IN THE NEW TESTAMENT

The New Testament is filled with references to five-fold ministry gifts. Apostles are mentioned 79 times. Prophets are mentioned 161 times. The term evangelist is used 3 times. The term pastor is used once and teacher is used 13 times.

The word "shepherd" is the same word as "pastor" in the Greek and it is used 18 times. It is never used as a title for any individual in the New Testament other than Jesus, Himself. Jesus is referred to as a shepherd 7 times. Other references deal with spiritual shepherds in general or literal shepherds of sheep.

There are at least twenty men in the New Testament referred to as apostles. Some were young apostles, like Timothy, apprenticing under Paul and others. There are also several people called prophets and teachers and one person who was called an evangelist. Jesus was the only individual in the New Testament who claimed the title of pastor.

The following verses from Acts are samples of these references:

*"So the **apostles** and **elders** came together to consider this matter." (Acts 15:6)*

*"Now in the church that was at Antioch there were certain **prophets and teachers**: Lucius of Cyrene, Manaen who had been brought up with Herod the tetrarch, and Saul." (Acts 13:1)*

*"Now Judas and Silas, themselves being **prophets** also, exhorted the brethren with many words, and strengthened them." (Acts 15:32)*

*"On the next day we who were Paul's companions departed and came to Caesarea, and entered the house of Philip the **evangelist**, who was one of the seven, and stayed with him. Now this man had four virgin daughters who **prophesied**. And as we stayed many days, a certain **prophet** named Agabus came down from Judea. (Acts 21:8-10)*

These verses are rich with information which helps us understand relationships within the five-fold ministries.

First of all, we know that certain men were clearly recognized as having specific ministries in the body. Some were called apostles, some prophets, some teachers and one is called an evangelist.

The second major point that we would like to highlight from these passages is that the title "pastor," as pointed out earlier, is lacking any specific application. We do notice the term "elder" used together with the apostles and we will look at this a little later and try to strengthen our case for the theory that these elders could also be called "pastors."

The third piece of information to notice is that individuals could hold more than one title or office in the church. Paul, as we know, was an apostle, but he was at that time numbered with the prophets and teachers. Philip was one of the seven deacons chosen in Acts 6, but he was also an evangelist. On the other hand, Agabus is mentioned twice in Acts, both times as a prophet.

A fourth bit of knowledge is that four young women prophesied, making it clear that this gift was not just for the men. Whether or not they prophesied in the church is not revealed, but is quite probable, since they had the reputation for prophesying.

The fifth thing we can note is that the ministry of prophets is to exhort and strengthen the brethren. This is consistent with I Corinthians 14, which focuses on the prophetic ministry and how useful it is to edify and build the body of Christ. Clearly, the gift is not to be self-serving or for personal kingdom building.

Purpose of All Five Ministry Gifts

The only place the five-fold ministry gifts are mentioned together is in Ephesians 4:11. This passage in its context gives us a very clear and significant statement about the purpose of all of these ministries. If we miss the message of Ephesians 4, we will have serious problems in inter-ministry relationships and we will never be able to do our part to fulfill God's agenda for these exciting days.

The context where we find these gifts listed is extremely important, beginning with the first verse of Ephesians 4. We are reminded of our high and holy calling that each of us has received. We are exhorted to walk worthy of this calling by staying humble, gentle and by doing our best to guard the unity of the Spirit. We are reminded that there is only one body, one Spirit, one hope of our calling, one Lord, one faith, one baptism and one God and Father of all.

We are reminded that David prophesied that when Jesus led captivity captive He gave gifts to men. (Psalm 68:18) Going back to the Old Testament source, we discover that God gave gifts to men, even to the rebellious, so that the Lord God might dwell among them.

He Dwells With Us Through His Gifts

There may not be any truth found in this passage which is more important than this: The gifts God gave to the church, including the five-fold ministry gifts, are given to the church so that He, Himself, can dwell among us. His passion has always been to be with His people, at the center of their life. In Exodus 25:8, God told Moses to have the people build Him a sanctuary, so that He could dwell among them. The sanctuary was placed in the center of the camp, surrounded by the twelve tribes, four in each direction. Throughout Scripture we read that God will dwell among His people. That is why in Revelation, when we reach the final stage of the history of God's creation, we read:

*"And I heard a loud voice from heaven saying, 'Behold, the tabernacle of God is with men, and **He will dwell with them**, and they shall be His people, and God Himself will be with them and be their God.'" (Revelation 21:3)*

The various spiritual gifts and ministries given by God to men are not primarily for the benefit of individual people, but are clearly for the purpose of allowing God to move freely among His own people and manifest His power and glory so that the whole world will become aware of His greatness and power. And of course, He wants the world to be saved and delivered from the power of sin and Satan, as a result of the revelation of His glory.

Spiritual gifts are the means by which God can still speak, heal, reveal, administrate, teach and love His creation. The five-fold ministries are leaders through whom the Holy Spirit works to do the work that Jesus did when He walked the earth in his mortal body.

Apostles administrate Jesus' own plans, bringing structure and order to the church.

Prophets speak the words that Jesus wants to speak to leaders and followers alike.

Evangelists are Jesus' feet going to the cities and villages to preach the gospel of the Kingdom of God.

Pastors reach out with Jesus' loving arms to heal and protect the little lambs and bring healing to the wounded.

Teachers reveal the liberating truths of the Kingdom that Jesus wants to teach His people. Now let's look at the passage which introduces the five-fold ministry concept.

*11. "And **He** Himself **gave** some to be apostles, some prophets, some evangelists, and some pastors and teachers,*

*12. **for the equipping of the saints for the work of ministry**, for the edifying of the body of Christ,*

13. till we all come to the unity of the faith and the knowledge of the Son of God, to a perfect man, to the measure of the stature of the fullness of Christ;

14. that we should no longer be children, tossed to and fro and carried about with every wind of doctrine, by the trickery of men, in the cunning craftiness by which they lie in wait to deceive,

15. but, speaking the truth in love, may grow up in all things into Him who is the head — Christ —

16. from whom the whole body, joined and knit together by what every joint supplies, according to the effective working by which every part does its share, causes growth of the body for the edifying of itself in love." (Ephesians 4:11-16)

Ephesians 4:11-16 is a six-verse sentence, with one main subject — God, and one main action verb — gave. All the rest of the phrases and clauses are given to add information and answer questions, such as why God gave, for how long He gave, etc.

A. Equipping the Saints

The first series of phrases, "for the equipping of the saints for the work of ministry" gives us one of the most important functions of all five gift-ministries, the function that facilitates the desire of the Lord God to dwell among us.

Church leadership must understand as never before that our divine mandate from Heaven is not primarily to build ministries or manifest spiritual gifts. It is to equip each and every saint to minister and serve the body of Jesus as vital members of that body which belongs to Him.

Equipping the saints must involve mentoring. Mentoring requires first discovering the giftings of each saint, so that those gifts can be properly developed. Discovering these giftings can be aided by good prophetic ministry. Developing these giftings requires mentoring by those who have like giftings.

Can Any Christian Rise to the Level of the Five-Fold Ministries?

I am well aware that I am very much in the minority, but my personal inclination is to believe that each of the saints has a gifting that could lead him or her into one of the five-fold ministry callings. That gifting needs to be developed and mentored, and the individual needs a deep desire to serve God. Clearly, there is already a great need for more leadership to equip the saints. This need will only increase as the world-wide revival, already in progress, spreads and grows around the world. This is how it will happen in my judgment.

When the evangelists are fully empowered by the apostles and prophets to fulfill their callings with the help of all the other ministries, there will always be many new converts to Christianity who need to be led into maturity. Thus there will always be a need for more mature leaders, which can most quickly be raised up through the mentoring process.

Mature apostles like Paul would be equipping young apostles like Timothy. Young prophets would hang out with older prophets just like the Old Testament "Schools of the Prophets" hung out with Elijah and Elisha. Evangelists would train other budding evangelists, and pastors and teachers would mentor those with like giftings. I believe that this is what Paul means when he says that the five-fold ministries were given for the equipping of the saints. Each one equips those who have similar callings.

It would be hard for an evangelist to equip a teacher, or vice-versa, although all Christians can learn some important principles of evangelism. Although I believe in specialization, I also believe that we can all learn to lead and organize, to speak prophetically, to evangelize, to love the sheep and to teach the young in the faith. But only a mature prophet can totally equip a young prophet to take his ministry to the level that God has in mind for him.

As mentioned earlier, the writer of Hebrews scolds the saints, saying that the time had come that they should be teachers. Instead they still needed the milk of the Word to be taught to them. They had other teachers teaching them, but they hadn't matured to become "teachers" themselves. Even so, Paul, when writing to Timothy, exhorted him to take what he had taught him, and teach the same to faithful men, who would be able to teach others also (II Timothy 2:2). **Mentoring was clearly the chosen method to equip the saints.**

Jesus also gave us the truth in Matthew 25:21, that declares that if we are faithful in a few things, He will make us a ruler over many things. I believe that if we are faithful to exercise the gifts of evangelism, teaching, pastoring, prophesying or overseeing, we will be given more and more authority and anointing in those gifts. I do believe that everyone has some gifting to do at least one of the five and those who are good stewards of these gifts will take them to a higher level. I do not believe that God would have us put a lid on someone's potential, by saying they can never attain to a certain level of responsibility. The more faithful we are, the more responsibility we will be given.

There are several other reasons for my belief that every Christian can move into one or more of the five-fold ministries.

1. "Each One" Principle

The first reason is that it is consistent with the repeated statement that He gave gifts to each one. The "each one" statement is found with each of the list of gifts, and this list in Ephesians 4:11-16 is no exception.

Notice that in Ephesians 4:7, Paul writes that *"each one was given grace according to the measure of the gift of Christ."* The next verse refers directly back to Psalm 68:18, which is here translated, *"Therefore He says, 'When He ascended up on high, He led captivity captive and gave gifts to men.' "*

Verse 9 and 10 are in parenthesis, dealing with Christ's descending and ascending. The very next verse, which in the context should be read directly after the one quoted above, is verse 11, which declares, *"And He, Himself, gave some apostles, some prophets, some evangelists and some pastors and teachers."*

Every other list of spiritual gifts in the New Testament indicates that each one fits somewhere in the list and I see no reason that this list is any exception, except for our tradition. If you read this passage in its contextual flow, leaving out the two verses which are in parenthesis, it should be quite clear. Also note the significance of the word, "Therefore," which begins verse 8. Paul first states that **each one** was given grace, (the essence of the gift) according to the measure of the gift of Christ. Then Paul says, "**Therefore** He says, . . . He gave gifts to men." The "therefore" has to refer to the "each one" receiving grace (the essence of the gift) in the preceding verse. It is hard to deny that Paul is implying that each one was given one of these gifts.

2. Scripture has no Clergy/Laity Dichotomy

Another reason to believe that each one has been given one of these gifts is that Paul's teaching on the body of Christ always focuses on the fact that each of us is a vitally important member. He never supports the concept of a "clergy—laity" dichotomy in the church. If we say some are called to be "five-fold level ministers" and others are just called to be "saints," it seems to me that we are slipping back into the "clergy—laity" concept.

I have seen and sensed this, even in our cutting edge apostolic movement, where there is still an unnecessary exaltation of the five-fold ministry, almost like the Hindu "Caste System." We imply that some are born to be rulers, and others are born to be followers or lower class citizens, even though we acknowledge that they can also be used of God in special ways.

Some of this attitude may come from our excessive historical exaltation of the ministry of the apostle. In spite of the fact that about twenty apostles are recognized in the New Testament, we have tended to ignore that fact and put the original twelve (minus Judas) on a very high pedestal. Only those long dead and gone, who are heroes of the Book of Acts could have been apostles. It is like what some groups have done with what we call sainthood.

Now that we are beginning to recognize the existence of these servants of God, we tend to still have an excessive reverence for the office. Since the other five-fold gift-ministries are grouped with the apostle, we tend to put them up on the same exalted level, that only a few can attain to.

3. All Of Us Have a High and Holy Calling

In the first verse of Ephesians 4 Paul exhorts the whole church to walk worthy of the calling that they have been given. He immediately follows with the reminder, just like in I Corinthians 12, that there is only one body, and one Lord, etc., but that to each one grace was given for the sake of that body.

Peter declares to the Jews of the dispersion, "You are a chosen generation, a royal priesthood, a holy nation." (I Peter 2:9). Revelation 1:6 and 5:10 both say that God has made us kings and priests. We are talking about some very exclusive positions in life but all of us are given these titles. Why should we put the five-fold ministry titles out of reach of God's kings and priests.

The picture is clear:

1. Everyone has a high and holy calling to edify and build up the one body of Jesus.
2. To each one was given grace according to the measure of the gift of Christ to fulfill that calling.
3. Some are given to the body of Jesus as apostles, some as prophets, some as evangelists, some as pastors and some as teachers.

Just as some have latent prophetic gifts or healing gifts and never use them, so some have apostolic or teaching gifts, who also never use them. But they can all be stirred up by leadership who come to encourage and fan the flames of their spiritual gifts.

Since writing most of this chapter, I have had the privilege of reading Bishop Bill Hamon's outstanding book, *"The Day of the Saints."* This powerful prophetic word predicts a coming explosion of ministry through ordinary "saints." Dr. Hamon (a pioneer prophet and apostle, whom I greatly admire) shares his conviction that the five-fold ministries will each equip and mentor the saints in their area of expertise. Like most Christian leaders, he doesn't see the saints themselves becoming five-fold leaders. But he does see all the saints doing great exploits for God, which would be very similar to what we would expect from those leaders that we would call fivefold ministers.

Although Dr. Hamon does not see the saints becoming five-fold ministers, he does see them maturing into powerful ministers of God. Perhaps the difference in viewpoint is just a difference in perspective. Dr. Hamon sees the saints being mentored and taught by the five-old ministries to do the work of the ministry. I see the saints being mentored into one of the five-fold ministries to do the work of the ministry.

Scripture, of course, gives us no clear definitions of these ministries, nor does it define a saint as opposed to a five-fold leader. We are left to speculate to some extent how to define these terms and how to distinguish the one from the other. The most important thing is not that we can define the terms, but rather that all five ministries fulfill their function on the earth and activate the whole body of Christ.

B. Edifying the Body of Christ

The first activity of the five-fold ministry, which we have discussed in some detail, is the equipping of the saints. The second activity of the five-fold ministries is the building or edifying of the body of Christ. They accomplish this not only by their own ministries, but also through those whom they have been equipping for service in the body. Verse 16 gives us a good picture of how this happens. Basically it is saying that each of the members of the body gets activated to fulfill his or her role in the body, using divinely given spiritual gifts. Thus the whole body gets built and strengthened to function the way it was created to function.

The more the body of Christ is whole and healthy and strong, the more Jesus will be doing again through us what He did when He walked here on the earth. In other words, people will be healed, delivered and taught the good news of the Kingdom of God. No one will be turned away, and all who come to the body of Christ will have their needs met in one way or another.

Unity

These gifts were given to men until we all come into the unity of the faith and the knowledge of the Son of God, to a perfect man, to the measure of the stature of the fullness of Christ. Obviously the above functions of equipping and building are designed to produce the unity in Jesus' body. **This then should be a major aspect of the vision and heart of the five-fold ministries. Apostles, prophets, evangelists, pastors and teachers should all have a focus of unity.**

Truth

Another purpose and function of the five-fold ministries is to establish the whole body in divine truth. This is also a function of all of the ministries, but especially that of the teachers, including those who could be called teaching apostles or apostolic teachers. Truth establishes the believers so they are not tossed about with every wind of doctrine and taken out by false teachers.

Love

As verse 15 declares, the goal is that believers speak the truth in love. Five-fold ministry leaders should be producing a healthy body that is filled with love that accompanies the truth. This of course should come first from the leaders, who are functioning in the "Agape" love of God, through the intimate relationship that they have with Him. That love should be passed on to each member of the body through the mentoring relationships that are developed in the body.

Growth

The result of all of the above is a very special kind of growth. Not just a growth in numbers of souls. That would be the bi-product. The goal is growing up in all things into Him who is the Head—Christ. This is a powerful concept. The word picture given here is that the body is under the Head, but not fully grown and thus not properly connected to the Head in many ways. Then as the five-fold ministries function in equipping, edifying, producing unity, and speaking the truth in love, the body begins to grow up in many areas of spiritual life, until little by little a strong connection is made by the body with its Head.

Verse 16 amplifies this thought and declares that from the resources of the Head, the whole body, with every member functioning, continues to grow and to build the body in love.

Undeclared Purpose of Growth

Paul goes on to exhort the Ephesians to walk with purpose and integrity, but he does not really state why God wants the five-fold ministries to produce the ultimate growth of the body. Perhaps it was because the answer should be obvious. Paul taught so often about the fact that the church is the Body of Christ, that perhaps he knew that they would instinctively know the answer.

We have already touched on the answer, but let us go into greater detail here. The body needs growth and strength and unity so that it can be used effectively by the Head. A stronger body can produce more work, and accomplish more of the desires of the Head. The head has little power to work without the aid of the body, and Jesus has chosen to make us His body.

The Healthy Body

When Jesus walked the earth, He had one human body to work through. When He ascended, He put His Spirit into His new body, the early church. In both of these situations, He had complete control over His body and it did everything He asked of it. After those early days, when they were all in one accord, divisions arose that were not readily resolved and the body of Jesus became somewhat less than God intended or created it to be.

The Body Deteriorates

The members of the body began to have more of a mind of their own, and communication from the Head to the extremities became more and more interrupted. Soon little earthly heads began to replace the supreme Head and the body divided into numerous little bodies with little heads. Sometimes the little heads listened to the Supreme Head, but other times they made their own decisions without consulting Him.

Quite recently God showed me a heart-breaking vision of the body of Christ. I was asking to see Jesus, but when I finally saw Him, I was not prepared for what I saw. I saw a crippled body in a wheel-chair. I couldn't see any detail, as everything was dark and foggy, but I knew that Jesus wanted me to remember the commission He had given me decades earlier to preach unity and healing to the body of Christ on the earth.

It's About Jesus

Summing up, we could simply say the following. The five-fold ministry concept is not about man and his gifts or his positions and functions in the body. Rather, **it's all about Jesus and His desire to make His love and salvation available to every human being on the face of the earth. It's about each of us having a part and a responsibility to express Him to the church and the world in the way that He wants to be expressed through us.**

It's not about us building better church organizations or making it into Charisma Magazine or some other publication. **It's about making Jesus famous, by letting Him use HIS OWN BODY to accomplish HIS OWN GOALS.** I don't know how to say it any clearer than that.

Chapter 4

KINGDOM ECONOMY

We will be talking about finances in a later chapter, but in this chapter we will be trying to lay out the economic system by which God makes provision of manpower and resources in the place where He wants them. Of course, He does this through His leadership, which He has equipped with His five ministry gifts.

Apostles and Pastors

The key leading players in the economy of God are the apostles and pastors, with prophets giving strategic input, as they hear from God. Pastors and apostles have quite distinct perspectives, as we will quickly see. First of all let us look at a biblical example of how they worked together.

In Acts 15, some of the Christian Jews came to Antioch and declared that the men must be circumcised if they wanted to be saved. Paul and Barnabas were there and disputed with them, but eventually they decided that they and certain others should go down to

Jerusalem to talk to the "apostles and elders" about the matter. As the story is told to us in chapter 15 and 16, the expression, "apostles and elders" is used a total of six times.

Interestingly enough, Luke never referred to the "apostles and prophets," who are called the foundation of the church. Rather, it is always the "apostles and elders." Again, I want to make the case that these "elders" were basically those called "pastors" in Ephesians 4:11. Both Paul and Peter, when addressing the elders, exhorted them to watch over the flock.

Paul told the "elders" of Ephesus:

*"Therefore take heed to yourselves and to all the **flock**, among which the Holy Spirit has made you **overseers**, to **shepherd** the church of God which He purchased with His own blood." (Acts 20:28)*

The elders are to be overseers of the flock, and they are to shepherd (or pastor) the church of God. Remember, there is only one word in Greek for shepherd and pastor. They are the same entity.

Peter wrote to the elders, identifying himself also as an elder:

*"**Shepherd** the **flock** of God which is among you, serving as **overseers**, not by constraint but willingly, not for dishonest gain but eagerly;" (I Peter 5:2)*

Notice both passages use identical terms, (words in bold) even though they are written by different writers. As we discussed earlier, the Hebrew elders sat at the gates of the city, guarding the entrance, like a shepherd at the door of the sheep fold. Even so, pastors are there to watch over the flock and oversee them.

I have not found anywhere in the New Testament where any other group of church leaders are exhorted in this way to watch over the sheep. Personally, I am satisfied that pastors in the Bible were the same people as those called elders. The two terms refer to different aspects of who they are, but they are the same individuals. Remember, that the apostles ordained elders in every church, and that none of the leaders of individual churches were ever called "Pastor." Rather, there were a number of elders (pastors) that were under the supervision of apostles.

At the same time, we reaffirm the statement that apostles are those who are sent out by God to administrate his Kingdom on the earth. First, they have spent some intensive time with Him, learning His ways and walking in His paths. They are sent to see that His Kingdom affairs are being taken care of wisely and that His Kingdom will grow as much as possible.

The Difference in the Perspective of the Apostles and Pastors

As we begin this section, please remember that when we speak of pastors, we are not speaking about the point person or chief executive officer of the church. We are talking about the person who has a gift to care for and nourish individual sheep, rather than the gifting to administrate a huge church or ministry.

God has called pastors to care about the health and welfare of the sheep. Jesus talked about Himself as the Good Shepherd, who gives His life for the sheep. In John 10, Jesus declares that the sheep know the Shepherd and He calls them by name. A true shepherd has a strong love and affection for each one of his sheep and they recognize his voice and find comfort and safety in his presence.

The fact that Jesus called Himself the Good Shepherd, should reassure us that the pastor is not a ministry of less importance than the apostle. Rather the pastor has a ministry of showing the love of Jesus on a one-on-one basis. He is not called to raise up huge congregations and administrate huge budgets. He is one of several in the church who are there to heal and comfort the hurting and to lead their flocks to the good pastures.

The pastor's overriding passion is the growth and welfare of each individual sheep and lamb in his flock. If they are sick, he wants them healed. If they are poor, he wants them to come into prosperity. If they are lost, he will seek and find them and bring them home to the fold.

Apostles, on the other hand, although they certainly love the sheep, (some may be former pastors and are now pastoral apostles) they do not know them all by name. Their focus is not on the individual sheep, but on the growth and expansion of the Kingdom of God. They see a much bigger picture and are much engaged in warfare against the armies of Satan. When God's Kingdom is being pushed backward by the enemy in some area, they want to recruit more soldiers to take back the possessions of their King and Master.

While teaching in Korea, I asked my students if they thought that "Pastor Cho" (leader of the world's largest church) knew the names of all his people. Of course, they laughed. I'm pretty sure that he doesn't even know the names of all the "associate pastors" in his church. There are several hundred of them. There is no doubt in my mind and heart that "Pastor Cho" is really "Apostle Cho," whether he likes the title or not. He and others in similar positions may be very "pastoral" in their gifting, but their calling is clearly "apostolic." Usually apostles are "pastors" to other pastors and leaders.

When the apostles move among the sheep, they are looking at them from the same perspective as the pastor, hoping to see that all the sheep are healthy, happy and contented. Rather, they are looking at the flock to see if there are any among them that are ready to be moved into a place of more responsibility to enlarge the Kingdom of God. Apostles will be asking the Holy Spirit to reveal the hearts and giftings of those they encounter, so that they can put them into the proper places of service for the growth of the Kingdom of God. They will work best in partnership with prophets that they know and trust.

The Kingdom Economic Cycle

With what we have just discussed, let us now look at how God's economic cycle works within the body of Christ. It involves all five ministries, but is driven chiefly by the distinctive passions of the pastors and apostles.

1. The process begins when the evangelist, who may also be apostolic or prophetic, fulfills his calling and brings some new little lambs into the house of God.

2. The little lambs stir up the instincts of the pastors, who gravitate to them like any normal mother does to a newborn baby. The pastors begin to nourish the lambs and involve the teachers who feed them some solid food and get them into a real growth mode. As the pastors notice the weaknesses and sicknesses among the sheep, they reach up into the storehouse of the Kingdom of God and give what is needed to their sheep.

The pastors minister the healing power of God to the sick. They reveal the principles of blessing and prosperity to those who are living in poverty. They bring the power of deliverance to those in bondages of the soul. In many cases, they will bring in specialists from among the extended body of Christ to help bring healing, prosperity as well as emotional and spiritual freedom to their sheep.

3. Teams of apostles and prophets begin to move among the flock, observing the growth of the lambs. Prophets begin to exhort and encourage them, and give them vision for their destiny in the Kingdom of God. Apostles make note of these prophetic declarations and keep their eyes on certain sheep, who seem to be the most mature and gifted among the flock.

When the apostle gets enough confirmation in his spirit, he may tell the pastor or pastors, that certain sheep are needed in a certain aspect of ministry. They will be placed under the mentorship of mature ministries with similar giftings. Many of the young sheep will be mentored by evangelists and given the exciting opportunity to evangelize people from the same lifestyle that they had previously been in.

Others will be placed with apostles, prophets, teachers or pastors. Each of the young ones will be given a limited amount of responsibility and discipled into maturity in their special gifting.

Apostles continue to follow and observe the most mature and gifted sheep and begin to plant them into various places of ministry, where their gifts can best be used, and where their weaknesses will be overcome. They do not leave them totally on their own, but will frequently check up on their progress.

4. As the new sheep progress into places of maturity and leadership, new lambs are being brought into the house at an increasing rate. This, of course, is because many of the first group of converts are now evangelists in their own right and are eagerly and aggressively invading every nook and cranny of society.

With the aid of supernatural gifts, such as the gifts of knowledge, wisdom, healings, faith, miracles, prophecy and discerning of spirits, these evangelists will bring the good news of Jesus' love to relatives, neighbors, classmates, teachers, coworkers, employees and employers. The results will be incredible growth. The cycle will continue as long as the leaders continue to guard the unity of the Spirit in the body of Christ, and keep their focus on the Kingdom of God rather than using the rapid growth for personal advantage or personal kingdom building.

5. The cycle continues with the creation of many additional sheepfolds and many new and younger pastors drawing from the wealth of the Kingdom of God to bring healing and prosperity to their little lambs. Older and younger apostles and prophets move among the young and maturing and encourage and inspire the lambs to grow into realms of ministry. And so the process continues until the whole world is turned upside down as it was in the book of Acts.

Let's simplify the picture.

1. Consider the hydrological cycle, the cycle of water evaporat-

ing from the ocean, forming clouds, falling as rain on the land, and returning to the ocean, to begin the cycle all over again.

In the same way, the pastor reaches up into the Heavens and pulls down the rain from heaven; that is the blessings of healing for the body and soul, prosperity for the poor and deliverance for those in bondage. **The pastor takes from the Kingdom of Heaven and gives to the sheep. Meanwhile the apostle surveys the flock and takes the wealth of the flock and puts it back into the Kingdom of Heaven.** It is like taking the water which has fallen from Heaven to water the earth and sending it back to the ocean of God's resources and love.

Thus the pastor wants to prosper the flock while the apostle wants to prosper the Kingdom. Of course, both of these ministries care about both of these entities, but their focus is mainly on the one which has become their chief responsibility.

2. Consider the financial cycle. Money is spent on goods and services. The money received is used to produce more goods and services than were originally created. Thus society is enriched. Raw materials become transformed into useful things when people add something to them, and someone's life is improved in some way. With each new product more resources are pulled into the cycle. And whenever something is produced and money changes hands, the economy grows a little bigger. When people stop spending, the economy slows and recession occurs.

The Kingdom of God is similar to this. The more raw materials (new converts) that are put into production, the more the Kingdom of God is enriched. When we draw the riches out of Heaven and put them into the raw materials from the earth, God's Kingdom will quickly grow. When Christians stop evangelizing, and when the five-fold ministries stop equipping the saints to be ministers, the economy of the Kingdom of God slows down and goes into recession.

Decision Making Process of theApostles and Elders

When Paul and Barnabas came to Jerusalem to get some answers regarding circumcision, it was the apostles and elders (pastors) who came together to make the decision for the church in Antioch. Again, we notice that it wasn't the prophets in this case that were teamed up with the apostles. Rather it was what I believe were the pastors. The question I asked was "Why?"

My personal (and strongly held) opinion is simply this. The leadership recognized the two perspectives of these two offices in the church. The apostles would represent the interests of the Kingdom of God and its expansion in the world. They would be very concerned that they would not slow down the growth of the church among the Gentiles.

On the other hand the elders (pastors) would have the concerns of their people in mind. They wanted to be assured that the sheep would not be hurt. I do believe prophetic people were also involved among the apostles and elders and that they gave some input into the discussion, but the weight of the decision fell on the shoulders of the apostles and elders.

This may seem like a very carnal comparison, but to me it is a lot like modern labor negotiations. Some of the negotiators represent the concerns of the management and others are from the union and represent the concerns of the employees.

We are aware of the fact that many church boards in the past have fought over various issues in similar ways that business and industry have fought over contracts. Basically, it is because different church members have different focuses and can not agree. That's where we need the work of the Holy Spirit to impart His understanding and wisdom to make decisions that will be healthy for both parties. In the passage in Acts 15, Peter, who called himself an elder, as well as an apostle, (He could be called a pastoral apostle.) seems to represent the concerns of the Gentile converts in his exhortation to the gathering.

Then Paul and Barnabas give an apostolic perspective as they recount what God did through them among the Gentiles, to give the local apostles and elders a broader picture of the growth of the church outside of Jerusalem. The effect was that the council would not want to slow the growth of the church among the Gentiles by adding rules and regulations from the Old Covenant.

James, an administratively gifted apostle, then declares his decision, based on the testimony already heard. He makes a very short list of rules that the Gentiles should obey and declares that the new converts should not be troubled by unnecessary regulations. Then the apostles and elders write a letter to the church with their decisions.

Now notice the wording in Acts 15:25 and 28. In verse 25, they wrote, "**It seemed good to us**, being assembled with one accord, to send chosen men to you with our beloved Barnabas and Paul," But in verse 28, they wrote, "**It seemed good to the Holy Spirit, and to us**, to lay upon you no greater burden than these necessary things:"

Regarding sending chosen men, they did what seemed good to them, but regarding the critical decisions made at their meeting, they did what seemed good to the Holy Spirit first. Here we have the prophetic element, which was not clearly expressed in their discussion, but was obviously at work in their meeting. They would not have made the statement that it seemed good to the Holy Spirit, if they had not heard from Him in some way.

At any rate, it was the apostles and elders (with probably some input from the prophetic people, including prophetic apostles), who made the decisions and protected both the new converts and the expansion of the Kingdom of God among the Gentiles. This seems to me to be a good precedent to follow in important policy-making decisions in the church.

Chapter 5

DEVELOPING SPECIALIZED MINISTRIES

As members of the body of Christ utilize their gifts more and more, they discover that they find it easier to flow in a certain direction with their gifts. They find they have more results in a certain vein of operation, while others will have better results in a different vein. This phenomenon is a result of God's plan to bring specialization into His church.

Many years ago in university I took a Developmental Psychology class. It was my introduction to DNA and genes. My professor explained that when the female cell is fertilized by the male sperm, the cells begin to divide. At first every cell is identical, but each one has the complete blueprint of the entire body.

As the cells continue to divide, they begin to take on different characteristics. Soon there are head cells, torso cells, arm cells and leg cells. As the cells continue to multiply in the proper way, more and more specialization occurs. Bone cells develop, eye and ear cells develop, finger and toe cells develop, each in the proper part of the body. Finally, every cell becomes highly specialized to do one specific job. Consider the many parts of the eye. Because each highly specialized cell functions in its proper place, the eye can see.

Even so in the body of Christ, we develop our gifts into a higher and higher state of specialization. At first, we try to do everything that Jesus did, with limited success. Then we find ourselves drawn into a more specific type of ministry, like music or speaking. As we develop and work with others, we find they may be more gifted in one aspect of music or speaking, while we lean toward a different aspect. I may find I like singing more than playing an instrument. Then I may discover my voice is higher than the other men who like to sing, so I sing the tenor part. But when another tenor has a higher voice than mine, he sings the first tenor, while I move to the second tenor part.

Another great analogy is the football team. Freshmen, who have never played football before may know that they like football, but don't know what position they would be best at. As they try out at different positions, they begin to find their niche. Some will join the offensive team, and others the defensive team. Some will discover they love playing on the line, while others love the thrill of carrying the ball. Some will desire to be the decision maker and play quarterback.

Football teams, have developed more and more specialized units and individuals over the years. Some are now punt return specialists. Some just kick field goals and others do the kick-off. Some go in on goal-line stands and others snap the ball for the punt or field goal try. Specialization continues to expand in football and other sports as well. In baseball we now have designated hitters, pinch hitters, pinch runners, starters, long relievers, short relievers and closers.

The medical field has seen more and more specialization, as everyone knows. Patients feel more confident going to a doctor, who is a specialist in his field, knowing that their physician has extra training and experience for their specific physical condition. A general practitioner may know about a lot of diseases and physical problems, but he can't know as much about any one particular condition as the specialist who has devoted his life to understanding that condition.

The fact is that the church seems to be far behind the world in this development, when we should be the leaders. We don't go to a dentist or a chiropractor to operate on our appendix, but we expect the person we call a pastor to have the answer to all our spiritual, physical, emotional and psychological problems.

We need to understand the teaching of I Corinthians 12 on the gifts of the Holy Spirit in the context of the body of Christ. The Bible never lists the gifts of the Holy Spirit without talking about the body of Christ. But I Corinthians 12 goes into great detail to make sure we understand that we all have specialized functions in the body of Christ.

Some of us are like eyes, some like ears, and some are hidden, yet important parts of the body. We can't get along without our liver or kidneys, or many other unseen organs, and even so the body of Christ needs all of us to do what He has called us to do. Some members of the body of Christ have powerful ministries far away from the spotlights on the church platform, and without them the ones on the platform would not be nearly as successful.

For instance, suppose a healing evangelist is being brought to the city to hold a healing crusade. The whole church community swings into action. Prophetic people give encouraging words to the leaders and workers, just like in the days of Ezra and Nehemiah. Administrators organize prayer meetings, advertising, worship and ministry teams and hundreds of other little details.

Intercessors begin to do spiritual warfare against the spirits that would oppose the crusade. They place a hedge of protection around the evangelist and the ministry team. They also pray earnestly for the power of the Holy Spirit to be released with healing gifts. They intercede for lost souls to be saved as a result.

The evangelists begin to spread out in the community and invite hundreds and thousands of people to attend, sharing their testimonies and their faith that God will touch each one who comes. People with gifts of helps do hundreds of little tasks, which receive little credit or honor on earth. Givers donate large sums of money to pay the many expenses.

Then the healing evangelist arrives. Someone has already made sure that he and his team have everything they need for accommodations, food and transportation. Soon the meetings begin. People are healed and delivered as the ministry team adds their gifts and anointings to the gifts and anointings of the evangelist, and many respond to accept Jesus as Lord and Savior as a result of the work of the Holy Spirit.

The apostolic leaders help guide the young converts to a flock where the best available pastors and teachers in the body will nourish and feed them first the milk and then the meat of the Word of God. As they begin to grow, they will be guided into more specific ministries through mentoring relationships. Soon they will be moving into serving as evangelists, intercessors, etc. Some will rise to positions of heavier administrative and spiritual responsibility and some will become specialists in prayer and evangelism. All of those who continue to follow the Lord and allow others to mentor them will grow wiser and more skilled in their specific specialty.

As various saints develop various specific gifts to a high level of proficiency, the whole body of Christ in the area will become aware of their gifts and spiritual skills. When a person in the body or out in the world has a need or a crisis in his life, people will know where to send him.

As we have listened to men and women of God with healing ministries and read their books, we find that many of them testify that they have more faith for certain kinds of afflictions than others. Some have great faith for cancer or diabetes. Others have a powerful healing ministry for back problems. Others see deaf or blind healed frequently and still others have faith to raise the dead.

Back to the Womb

We began this chapter talking about the growth of a baby in the womb. We stated that each cell had the blueprint of the entire body in its DNA. Each Christian has the DNA of Jesus and is a part of the whole body.

When there are still only a few cells, none of them are very specialized. In a small church with only a few members, most members have to fill several positions. They do not have the privilege of specialization. But as the body grows, the individual members, like the individual cells, can focus more and more on specific functions in the body.

Each of us have the potential to become more and more skilled in some area of ministry, if we recognize that there are other members of the body who can do some of the things we do. In fact, if we give them time to mature and specialize in those things, they may well become better than we are at them.

This is of course, the principle of teamwork. Whether baseball, football, soccer, hockey or basketball, specialization leads to greater success for the team. So it is in the Kingdom of God. We might enjoy a bigger variety of ministries and not want to yield to a younger person, but we will never get as good as we could be at one thing if we try to do ten.

Many great men and women of God have actually shipwrecked their ministries by doing more than what God wanted them to do. One outstanding prophet with a great healing ministry in the mid-nineteen hundreds insisted on trying to become a teacher and theologian, as well as a prophet. He not only went off the deep end himself, but led many people to follow his foolishness, because they felt that a man with such a great anointing couldn't be wrong. He fell from a place of being a humble servant to a place of deriding all those who disagreed with him. God took him home early in an automobile accident.

Another great man of God earlier in the century also had a powerful ministry, but let many other projects sidetrack him from what God had called him to do. He also lost his effectiveness and wounded the body of Christ. Both of these men had problems submitting to anyone. As prophets, they should have listened to the apostles God had given to them for relationships. On the other hand, if they were functioning as apostles, they should have had prophetic people confirming what they were doing or preaching. Again, we re-emphasize the fact that prophets and apostles need each other.

There are times when we need to fill roles that are not our specialty. Many times God actually puts us in places where we can develop skills that are not our primary ministry. God often uses apostolic leaders and pastors to put us in places like that to shore up some weak areas and give us a little experience to help us understand others. Then He will allow us to move back into our main giftings and begin to perfect them.

Chapter 6

FINANCING THE
FIVE-FOLD MINISTRIES

This chapter may be somewhat controversial. My goal is always to bring unity and not to offend my brothers and sisters in Christ, but I believe that the issue of financing Kingdom expansion through full use of the five-fold ministry must be openly and honestly addressed. We will first examine our present financing process and what its advantages and limitations are. Then we will try to visualize a more biblical and effective model to finance the harvest of souls. Our goal is to stimulate the leadership of the body of Christ to ask the right questions and to be willing to kill one of the most sacred of all Christian cows—how we receive our money from ministry.

Of course, we are not focusing on how to finance our own personal ministry. Rather, we are focusing on how to finance the harvest. Unfortunately, these are not necessarily the same thing.

I also want to make it very clear that my motives for writing any of the following chapter have nothing to do with my present position of service in the Kingdom of God. I love this walk of faith that God has called us into. It is far more exciting than living on a predictable salary, with lots of insurance and financial security. In this walk we expect no regular income, so every blessing that we receive is like Christmas, and it comes so often in specific answer to specific prayer.

Of course, what I prefer is not necessarily the pattern for the Kingdom of God at large. As always, we want to examine every related Scripture to learn about the biblical pattern for financing the Kingdom of God and draw whatever conclusions we can about the subject. Then we must seek for wisdom to know what will and what will not work in our present society.

How is Money Normally Raised and Distributed in the Church Today?

1. Denominational churches

Churches of most denominations get some help from their headquarters when they start a new work. They also are expected, as they grow, to give back to their denominational leadership a certain portion of their income to finance the administration of the denomination. It may be 10% or some other figure.

The way the church raises its money is usually through taking collections of the people's tithes and offerings. What they receive is normally distributed with the following priorities: First, whatever the denominations requires; second, the bills of the local church are paid; third, the "pastor" or "pastors" are paid a designated salary. Most churches also have a missionary budget, which is usually promoted and partially administrated by the denomination. Many have an ongoing building fund and possibly a benevolent fund for charity in the community.

Itinerant ministries may be brought in occasionally to bring specialized ministry to the local church. This is usually coordinated by the district office of the denomination. Support for the traveling ministry, usually comes from special offerings taken up by the church, which may be an expense offering and/or a love offering. In many cases, the church will give a predetermined honorarium. Some evangelists actually require a specific amount plus travel expenses before they come. The traveling minister, in turn, will give a portion of his income, perhaps a tithe, back to the denomination.

2. Local independent churches

The independent churches, which have no denominational headquarters, vary only slightly from their denominational counterparts. Basically, they operate the same way, except there is no exchange of support with their denominational headquarters. Their missionary support may be partial support of a number of missionaries, or if their budget is large enough, and they have the vision for it, they may support numerous missionaries single-handedly.

Itinerant ministries, who are often also independent, are called in when the church feels that their coming will bring blessing and growth to their congregation. Compensation is usually similar to that in denominational churches. The traveling minister will be paid an honorarium, or the church will take up a special love offering for him or her. Often, traveling expenses will be paid separately.

3. Para-church ministries

Many different services to the body of Christ are provided by what are often called "Para-church ministries." These include Christian radio and TV stations and networks, men's ministries and women's ministries, campus and youth ministries, mission organizations, anti-abortion movements, and traveling ministries of all kinds, including music groups, drama teams and even comedians.

Most of these ministries must find creative ways to bring in their financial resources. Only if they are successful in this endeavor will they survive in ministry. They are usually constrained by church leaders that it violates biblical principles to accept the tithes of Christians, as those belong solely to their local churches. As a result they are totally dependent on Christians who are willing to go the extra mile and give an offering over and above their tithes.

Positive Aspects of Our Present System

There are some real positive aspects of our present system which we want to acknowledge. One of the most beneficial is that for the most part, those ministries that really produce results will remain in ministry. There is no tenure or guaranteed salary for those who think they should be "in the ministry," but have nothing relevant to offer to the body of Christ.

Another positive aspect of our present system is that most of the needs of the church and the world are addressed at some level. Most denominations and large independent churches cover the basic ministry needs that exist in our world, and the multitude of para-church ministries address most of the rest of them. Let us now look at some of the down sides of our system.

What Are the Limitations of Our Present System?

1. Important five-fold ministries may lack financing.

Since the local church and denominational leaders control almost all of the incoming tithe and a good part of the offerings, the vision of the leadership of these entities will determine how the incoming money will be spent. This is a good thing when the leadership of the church has God's vision, which is balanced and comprehensive. But **if most of the leaders in control of finances have the same basic gift or burden, other areas may be neglected.**

For instance, when most of the money is controlled by those with the five-fold ministry gift of "pastor," their priority with the money will be to care for the sheep they presently have. That may include adding more "pastors" for the various needs of the body, such as children, youth, singles, married couples and the elderly.

There are always many needs in the body and often not enough finances to go around. The pastor loves his sheep and wants them to be strong and healthy. Ministries brought in will be to help him care for the sheep, because he loves them so much. I know this from experience, having functioned as a pastor for many years. God has given him a love for the sheep and he is doing what his gifting demands. He wants to win souls but he is kept so busy caring for the sheep and their needs that there is little time or money to channel into evangelism or other Kingdom building projects.

As we have seen, the evangelist, whose passion is to win souls, is a vital dynamic in the growth and expansion of the Kingdom of God. If he is not first affirmed, and then mentored and financed, the church will become inward-focused rather than focused on Kingdom expansion.

The prophets in the midst, who often are not great administrators or leaders, may not find the pastors very open to what they have to say. The pastors also may not see the importance of supporting someone who seems to have few "practical" gifts and whose main purpose is to listen to God's voice and speak words to people whenever he feels led.

Those highly gifted as teachers may find themselves receiving income by teaching in Bible Colleges or seminaries. Others may teach Sunday School or they may even function as "pastor" of a local church. Their churches may grow if they are strong teachers, but the church may be weak in other outreach ministries, unless they are multi-gifted or good administrative leaders, as well as teachers. In that case they will find others to fill in for their weaknesses.

Many churches and denominations are actually run by those with apostolic giftings, but they are usually called pastors or presidents or superintendents, etc. A strong apostle will often receive a ministry salary in one form or another, by virtue of his anointing, but if he is not recognized and affirmed in his particular office, he will not be released to really function as an apostle. He may not even understand what he has actually been called to do. But because he feels called and sent by God, he does what one normally does and becomes a "pastor" or an evangelist or a missionary, etc.

Because only "pastors" and a few other administrators receive regular salaries in the present system, most itinerant ministries and para-church ministries must spend much time and energy raising the money they need to continue to function. Those who get skillful at bringing in the finances survive, and those who don't, often fold. While often it is also those who really touch people that survive, sometimes some very worthy ministries have to cut back or quit what they are doing because of financial realities. Some of these precious folk minister to the lower classes of society, where they receive very little financial help from those to whom they minister. If they have no forum to publicize their ministry, they may struggle to continue because of a lack of funds.

We see a real parallel in Scripture. In Nehemiah 13:10, we read that the Levites and singers, who should have been serving in the temple, had gone back to their fields, because of a lack of finances. Earlier in the history of Judah, King Hezekiah commanded the citizens of Jerusalem to contribute support for the priests and Levites so they could "devote themselves to the Law of the Lord." (II Chronicles 3:4)

2. Fundraising by some ministries gives Christianity a black eye.

Unfortunately, leaders of para-church ministries are human like everyone else, and if they discover that they have a gift to get people to respond to their appeals for funds, they might find it difficult not to use that fund-raising ability for personal advantage or to build their ministry to a new level. They find ways to justify their methods, and sometimes find themselves using a little exaggeration to make their appeals a little more appealing. They may see a great opportunity for expansion of their ministry or they may suddenly experience increasing financial pressure. These may lead them to find more creative ways to manipulate people's emotions.

While their techniques may work on many of their listeners and supporters, others who hear their appeals get suspicious of their motives and may begin to stir up opposition to their ministry. When people outside the church listen to them, they may judge them to be charlatans, manipulating people to get their money.

Of course, many keep their hearts and methods pure, and trust God to keep them going. They use the most honorable methods available to finance their ministries, and God honors them in the long run. The tragedy is that it only takes a few highly visible ministries, who compromise their integrity, to give all evangelists or TV hosts a bad name. How vividly we saw this in the past two decades, especially the 1980's.

The fact is that we give "pastors" a salary, but most other ministries are given income according to their ability to motivate people to give. It's interesting to note that very few regular "pastors" have come into disrepute because of their handling of finances, compared to evangelists and para-church ministries.

3. Christians feel the pressure as many ministries compete with each other for their support.

Just as people get weary of phone calls from telemarketers, many saints of God have gotten weary of financial appeals from the hundreds of para-church ministries that are in competition with each other as well as with their local churches for the free-will offerings they hope to receive from sympathetic saints. Incidentally, while reading to edit this chapter, I received a phone call from a para-church ministry, asking if I would like to become a partner.

Those attending denominational churches are often encouraged to give it all to their own denomination, where they know that their money is going to ministries that they can trust. While pastoring a denominational church part time during my seminary years, our district and national overseers urged us to tell our people not to support other missions, but to support our own mission endeavors.

Even large independent churches have many faceted ministries that cover almost every known aspect of outreach. They also would prefer that their people would trust them with their offerings as well as their tithes, because they are trying to do so many things on a limited budget.

But today the world is getting smaller and walls that keep people in their own little church world are coming down. Almost every Christian is exposed to the cry for help from a variety of ministries outside of their own church or denomination. Perhaps it's time to think about a transformation of our financial system in the church, the body of Christ. Could there be a better way that won't bring such stress to the body of Christ from the competition over finances.

While working on this chapter, I heard a television preacher declare that he was counseled by professional financial consultants, who work with Christian ministries. He had already partially paid them for their services, when they advised him to do things that were deceitful and dishonest in order to get more money from people. It involved making emotional appeals, using pictures of starving children, etc. He didn't even have a ministry to starving children, but that didn't matter to them. Of course, he rejected their proposals, but they acted like their methods were just normal for television ministries. He acknowledged that his ministry needed the extra income and struggled financially for some time, but God has honored his integrity with greater prosperity and blessings.

In spite of the limitations of our present system, we want to again acknowledge that much is still being done through the five-fold ministries that God has put in the church. The spiritual energy within each of these ministries comes out in one way or another, even though it may not be channeled in the most efficient way. But I believe that when we not only recognize the different giftings, but also begin to release the finances in the appropriate way, we will see an increase in the growth of the church in truly biblical proportions.

In Search of a Biblical Model of
Financing the Five-Fold Ministries

The challenge we face in trying to establish a biblical model for our present-day church is that there were no denominations or para-church ministries in the biblical era. There was basically only one church. Divisions within the church were appearing, but they were quickly challenged and rebuked by Paul and others.

The good news is that walls that divide today's church are breaking down. God is bringing us rapidly towards a level of unity of the Spirit, which we have not seen since biblical times. As this unity progresses in the days ahead, I believe that our system of financing the five-fold ministry will also progress toward a more biblical model. What then is the biblical model?

A. FROM THE BOOK OF ACTS

The **first** reference to finances in Acts is the following:

"Now all who believed were together, and had all things in common, and sold their possessions and goods and divided them among all, as anyone had need." (Acts 2:44, 45)

Here we discover that immediately after the very first spontaneous and powerful manifestation of the Holy Spirit; which was followed by the very first spontaneous and powerful message by Peter; which was then followed by the first great harvest of souls; the people had a powerful mind to give. In this passage it appears that the people gave to one another as soon as they saw someone with a need, without going through the church leadership. They did not wait for the church to meet the needs, they did everything they could to meet them with their own resources.

The **second** reference reveals a different twist:

"Now the multitude of those who believed were of one heart and one soul; neither did anyone say that any of the things he possessed was his own, but they had all things in common. And with great power the apostles gave witness to the resurrection of the Lord Jesus. And great grace was upon them all. Nor was there anyone among them who lacked; for all who were possessors of lands or houses sold them, and brought the proceeds of the things that were sold, and **laid them at the apostles' feet***; and they distributed to each as anyone had need. And Joses, who was also named Barnabas by the apostles (which is translated Son of Encouragement), a Levite of the country of Cyprus, having land, sold it, and brought the money and* **laid it at the apostles' feet***." (Acts 4:32-37)*

Here we have the same unselfish commitment to one another, with the sharing of all possessions, but now we see that at least the larger donations were brought to the apostles and laid at their feet. I believe that as we further examine the biblical record we will discover that the key to a better way of financing the harvest is through the affirmation and empowering of apostles, who are gifted with the ability to look at the whole picture and decide where the money should be spent.

The **third** reference reaffirms the previous:

"But a certain man named Ananias, with Sapphira his wife, sold a

possession. And he kept back part of the proceeds, his wife also being aware of it, and brought a certain part and laid it at the apostles' feet. But Peter said, 'Ananias, why has Satan filled your heart to lie to the Holy Spirit and keep back part of the price of the land for yourself?' " (Acts 5:1-3)

This is the third time the expression is used "laid it at the apostles' feet." In this story we see the wisdom of money being brought to the apostles, rather than to other ministries, which were possibly not as gifted with divine authority. Rather than being excited that he could finance another church project, Peter was able to discern the lying spirit and was given a word of knowledge to bring divine justice and to keep the church pure and united for a little longer. It would be interesting to know what the apostles did with the donation of the "deceitful duo," but we are not told.

The **fourth** reference adds another development:

"Now in those days, when the number of the disciples was multiplying, there arose a murmuring against the Hebrews by the Hellenists, because their widows were neglected in the daily distribution. Then the twelve summoned the multitude of the disciples and said, 'It is not desirable that we should leave the word of God and serve tables. Therefore, brethren, seek out from among you seven men of good reputation, full of the Holy Spirit and wisdom, whom we may appoint over this business; but we will give ourselves continually to prayer and to the ministry of the word.' " (Acts 6:1-4)

This passage doesn't mention money or giving; rather it deals with the distribution of funds and goods which had already been donated and laid at the apostles' feet. Notice that the apostles administrated the problem, and had the people choose men who were "full of the Holy Spirit and wisdom." These "deacons" supervised the distribution of goods, but they operated under the oversight of the twelve apostles.

A **fifth** reference to giving and receiving is that of Cornelius, the first Gentile convert. He was known as a man who *"feared God with all his household, who gave alms generously to the people and prayed to God always." (Acts 10:2).* We have no record of any of his gifts to the church after his conversion and experience with the Holy Spirit, but we do know that he was a generous giving person. He was visited by an angel who gave him the following declaration:

"Your prayers and your alms have come up for a memorial before God." (Acts 10:4)

What we learn from this passage is simply that generous giving, along with prayer, is honored and rewarded by God. It doesn't give us any insight into the giving and distribution for the support of the fivefold ministry, but it does remind us that God loves and blesses cheerful givers. Without the spirit of giving in the church, there will be no financing of the coming harvest.

The **sixth** reference to giving is in the following chapter:

"And in these days prophets came from Jerusalem to Antioch. Then one of them, named Agabus, stood up and showed by the Spirit that there was going to be a great famine throughout all the world, which also happened in the days of Claudius Caesar. Then the disciples, each according to his ability, determined to send relief to the brethren dwelling in Judea. This they also did, and sent it to the elders by the hands of Barnabas and Saul. (Acts 11:27-30)

This passage is interesting for more than one reason. First of all, we see the spontaneous nature of the giving of the early church. There was a need, so each one gave as they were able and the gift was sent by respected leaders, who were first numbered with a group of prophets and teachers, but who were soon to become known as apostles.

The second interesting point is that their giving was in response to a word from a recognized fivefold ministry prophet. Through the ministry of Agabus, the church was informed in advance and the need was addressed before it took place. This is a powerful five-fold ministry dynamic that we can expect to be restored, as we acknowledge and affirm all five ministries again.

The **seventh** reference to financing the ministry is in Acts 20. Paul concludes his exhortation to the Ephesian elders with this declaration:

> *"I have coveted no one's silver or gold or apparel. Yes, you your-selves know that **these hands have provided for my necessities, and for those who were with me.** I have shown you in every way, by laboring like this, that you must support the weak. And remember the words of the Lord Jesus, that He said, 'It is more blessed to give than to receive.'" (Acts 20:33-35)*

The time-frame of this passage is many years after Pentecost. It is just before Paul's arrest in Jerusalem. By this time, the church's unity and vitality have been seriously damaged, even though the church has grown in number and has expanded to many regions of the world. Divisions and false teachings have invaded, and the zeal for giving has also declined. Paul warned the Ephesian elders of wolves that would come and wound the flock and draw away disciples after themselves. (Acts 20:30) Combined with Paul's clear statement about how he supported himself and his team, this Scripture indicates things are quite different at this point of time.

What we do learn from this scripture is that as an apostle, Paul took the leadership to see that the financial needs of his team were met. He also found it necessary to do some teaching about finances, making himself as an example that they could follow. Later on we will see in the epistles that Paul had the right to ask for finances as an apostle, but he would rather support himself and let others give freely to support him, than to ever demand his rights as an apostle.

There are no more clear references anywhere in Acts to the receiving and distribution of finances in the early church. What we have then are the following five nuggets of truth in this regard.

1. People give spontaneously to each other after a visitation by God.
2. People sell significant possessions and give proceeds to apostles.
3. Apostles ordain deacons to administrate food among widows.
4. A prophet predicts famine. Antioch Christians send support as each is able.
5. Paul works rather than demanding support for himself and his team.

What is the significance of this limited information? Have we learned anything that applies to our investigation? I believe these five nuggets of information are very valuable in adjusting our vision of how to finance the harvest of souls, which is ripening so quickly. Four points stand out.

1. The first point is that unless the people have a heart to give, we won't have a lot of finances to administrate and ministries will continue to compete for the available ministry resources. But what gives people a heart to give? Today, we use two main methods to motivate giving.

First, we try to stir up people's emotions. We often appeal to their compassion to help the needy, or to their feelings of guilt for not doing more to support the church. This may involve an appeal to their sense of responsibility and morality and a legalistic type of teaching on tithes and offerings.

Second, we motivate people to give by appealing to their own self-interest. We quote numerous Scriptures such as "give and it shall be given to you" and many others which refer to sowing and reaping in both Old and New Testament passages. People are taught that giving is a way to solve their own financial problems. Most people are struggling with finances and it often gets their attention.

I am not criticizing these methods per se. People do need to be taught basic laws of finances and biblical principles relating to success and prosperity. But I am simply stating that in the absence of exuberant enthusiasm, such as was found in "Early Acts," (the early days of the early church) we often get pressured into various means of manipulating people to keep our ministries running.

The key question is, "Why did the Christians in 'Early Acts' have such a passion to give?" My answer would be the following:

The people had seen a demonstration of the power of God through leaders who had been with Jesus, and carried his authority. The power of the Holy Spirit was on the apostles in such a powerful way that the people saw the power of Jesus in them. At the same time they saw a humility, and a sincere commitment to give the glory to Jesus, rather than themselves. The humble, unselfish Spirit of Jesus

had filled the apostles, and was transferred to those who were drinking in the same Spirit in their presence. Many had just received salvation and others may have been healed of incurable diseases. They were primed to give.

First the people wanted to give to everyone they saw in need, just as Jesus had. Then they wanted to do more and sold their possessions and goods. When their neighbors' needs were met, they gave everything to the apostles, so their trusted leaders could do whatever God wanted them to do.

2. The second point is this: People will give with more confidence and freedom when they are led by apostles, rather than other gift-ministries, such as pastors. As apostles are being released and empowered to truly function as apostles, and as they come together in relationships with other apostles and prophets, there will be an explosion and release of the supernatural power of signs and wonders. This will trigger a passion for giving among the people and especially among those who are financial and business leaders. These people recognize leadership ability and are very discerning of character and integrity or the lack of it, because they have been burned too many times in business. They are looking for something that will be a secure eternal investment. They are tired of ministries that try to manipulate them for support.

I personally believe that when the time is right, we will see a repetition of "Early Acts." People will never have to be asked to give. Giving will be extremely contagious and people will once again sell major possessions to empower the Kingdom of God.

But let me restate this in the famous words of John Maxwell, "Everything rises and falls on leadership." When the leadership is under the control of wise and committed apostles, working with true prophets, wonderful things take place, and finances begin to flow. One only has to observe those ministries who are growing rapidly and have a strong financial flow. They have apostolic leaders and they listen to prophetic advisors before making major decisions. This truth is confirmed in at least three books written by Dr. C. Peter Wagner. They are *"The New Apostolic Churches," "Apostles and Prophets,"* and *"Churchquake."*

3. The third point is that the distribution of funds should be delegated to those who are full of the Spirit of God but under the administrative eyes of the apostles. One of the things we notice in Scripture is that there seemed to almost always be a plurality of ministries working together. In the early church, it was always "the apostles," not just one apostle making a major decision. There were groups of prophets and teachers working together. The "elders" were called from Ephesus. Probably the only exception was Philip, the evangelist and deacon, who went first to Samaria and then to Gaza to evangelize the Ethiopian eunuch. His ministry was specialized and did not include major decision-making authority, other than obedience to God's voice.

At any rate, we notice that Apostles made the decision as to how to handle administrative problems. They involved the people in finding the solution, asking them to chose seven anointed men, but the apostles did the commissioning and approving of the seven. Again, apostles administrated the Kingdom of God on the earth, and they did it as a group. This gave people confidence that their gifts would be spent wisely.

4. The fourth point is that the church listened to prophets and gave in response to prophetic revelation, under supervision of apostles. We are told in Acts 11 that Barnabas brought Saul to Antioch. Then a group of prophets came, one of them being Agabus, who prophesied a famine. The disciples, the saints in Antioch, determined to send help to Jerusalem. Barnabas and Saul took their gifts back to Jerusalem. What is clear here is that giving was again a clear response from the heart of the people to something God was doing, rather than the manipulation of their emotions. Everyone gave according to their honest ability and apostolic leaders oversaw its distribution.

5. The fifth point is that when enthusiastic giving wanes, even apostles may end up working to support themselves and their teams, but they prefer never to demand support, but rather to work and trust God. The unfortunate result is that these apostles did not have the luxury of "giving themselves to prayer and the ministry of the Word." Instead they had to work for their own support, like the Levites in the days of Nehemiah, etc. Paul could probably have moved around and spent more time in churches which supported him more readily, but he chose to follow the leading of the Lord and spend time where the need was the greatest.

B. REFERENCES TO FINANCES IN THE EPISTLES

As we look into the epistles, we will keep in mind that the condition of the churches when the epistles were written was quite different than what we read about in the first few chapters of Acts. Decades had passed, and much of the original fervor had cooled off. Still, the church was the most powerful force in the world and was invading the kingdom of man on a thousand different fronts, until it was said that the Christians had "turned the world upside down." We will include all passages that deal with collection and distribution of finances, as well as other references to the subject of money. We will try to summarize some of the lengthier passages to keep this study from getting too long.

Romans

We find three related references in the book of Romans. The first is an indirect reference to finances:

*"How then shall they call on Him in whom they have not believed? And how shall they believe in Him of whom they have not heard? And how shall they hear without a preacher? **And how shall they preach unless they are sent?**" (Romans 10:14, 15)*

This verse with its context clearly speaks of the ministry of the evangelist. Although part of the sending of the evangelist would include prayer and prophetic encouragement, I believe the above highlighted statement is clearly talking about financial provision for the journey. Although Jesus sent his disciples on missions with instructions to trust God for provision from those they ministered to, we know that Paul, at this stage, was being provided for through the churches or his own labor. I also believe that when Paul and Barnabas were first sent out, there was financial support along with the prophetic encouragement.

"Distributing to the needs of the saints, given to hospitality." (Romans 12:13)

This verse comes in the middle of a list of exhortations which follow a list of gifts often called the "Motivational Gifts." It exhorts individuals to take personal responsibility for caring for the needs of others, rather than leaving it all to the church leadership.

The next passage reveals a basic New Testament principle of giving.

"For it pleased those from Macedonia and Achaia to make a certain contribution for the poor among the saints who are in Jerusalem. It pleased them indeed, and they are their debtors. For if the Gentiles have been partakers of their spiritual things, their duty is also to minister to them in material things." (Romans 15:26, 27)

Both of these last two references refer to generosity and caring for the poor. The latter passage also indicates a moral duty to support financially those who provide spiritual blessings.

I Corinthians

The first of many related references in Paul's first letter to Corinth is this:

*"Even to the present hour we both hunger and thirst, and we are poorly clothed, and beaten, and homeless. And **we labor, working with our own hands**. Being reviled, we bless; being persecuted, we endure it;" (I Corinthians 4:11, 12)*

Paul is establishing that he is willing to go without, or work on the side, in order that the Corinthians might be made rich. This should not be the norm for apostles, but they should love the Kingdom of God enough to make that sacrifice when necessary.

Paul devotes most of the ninth chapter of I Corinthians to the fact that he has a clear right to enjoy financial rewards from his ministry. He declares:

> *"Do you not know that those who minister the holy things eat of the things of the temple, and those who serve at the altar partake of the offerings of the altar? Even so the Lord has commanded **that those who preach the gospel should live from the gospel.**" (I Corinthians 9:13, 14)*

He quickly adds his next comment:

> *"But I have used none of these things, nor have I written these things that it should be done so to me; for it would be better for me to die than that anyone should make my boasting void. For if I do this willingly, I have a reward; but if against my will, I have been entrusted with a stewardship. **What is my reward then? That when I preach the gospel, I may present the gospel of Christ without charge, that I may not abuse my authority in the gospel.** For though I am free from all men, I have made myself a servant to all, that I might win the more;" (I Corinthians 9:15-19)*

In this Scripture we find Paul demonstrating the character of Jesus, at the same time as he is teaching the people what their correct response should be. This should be an example to leaders in times when the people don't have the proper motivation to give. Paul was concerned that he wouldn't abuse his apostolic authority, so he made himself a servant instead of a dictator in the hope that more people would see the love of Jesus in him and accept Him as their savior.

The next passage is likewise powerful and insightful:

> *"Now **concerning the collection for the saints,** as I have given orders to the churches of Galatia, so you must do also: On the first*

day of the week let each one of you lay something aside, storing up as he may prosper, that there be no collections when I come. And when I come, whomever you approve by your letters I will send to bear your gift to Jerusalem. But if it is fitting that I go also, they will go with me." (I Corinthians 16:1-4)

Here we have the first use of the word "collections." Paul told the churches of both Galatia and Corinth to take up a collection on the first day of the week. He didn't use the word tithe, but he did say to give in proportion to their income. Again we find **apostolic administration of finances** in this passage. In the absence of great enthusiastic giving, Paul was providing apostolic leadership in this important part of Christian living.

Strangely enough, Paul didn't want any collection taken while he was there. This really is contrary to our custom. We normally take up the biggest offering when the biggest preachers attract the biggest crowds. The other interesting fact is that the offerings were not for Paul, but rather for the poor in Jerusalem. He does remark that he may accompany whomever they choose to carry the money to Jerusalem, indicating another aspect of apostolic supervision of finances.

II Corinthians

In the book of II Corinthians we find very little about finances until the eighth and ninth chapters, which go into great detail on the subject. Paul begins the eighth chapter praising the churches of Macedonia for their great generosity:

*"that in a great trial of affliction the **abundance of their joy** and their deep poverty abounded in the **riches of their liberality**. For I bear witness that according to their ability, yes, and beyond their ability, they were freely willing, imploring me with much urgency*

*that we would receive the gift and the fellowship of the minister-
ing to the saints. And this they did, not as we had hoped, **but first
gave themselves to the Lord, and then to us by the will of
God. So we urged Titus, that as he had begun, so he would
also complete this grace in you as well.**" (II Corinthians 8:5)*

Important points from this passage are the following: The **first**
point is that they had abundant joy, which even with deep poverty,
produced riches of liberality. Joyful Christians give much more willingly than discouraged Christians, and those experiencing the power
of God through anointed leaders, usually are much more joyful.

The **second** significant point is that joyful Christians, who have
seen the glory and power of God touch and bless them, give themselves more completely to God and are more committed to the work
of the Lord. They also commit themselves to the leadership, as we
saw in our study of "Early Acts."

The **third** point is that the Apostle Paul instructed Titus, also an
apostle (check II Corinthians 8:23 in the Greek), to teach the Corinthians this "grace" of giving joyfully.

Later in the eighth chapter Paul makes the point that giving
to those in need, when they have the means to help, will result in
them becoming the recipients when they, themselves, have a need,
providing an "equality." He uses the word "equality" twice in verse
14 of this discussion. Chapter nine discusses being prepared to give
and then following through with their good intentions by actually
making the donation they had planned to give.

Then Paul discusses the well known principle of sowing and
reaping, proclaiming that:

*"He who sows sparingly will also reap sparingly, and he who sows
bountifully will also reap bountifully. **So let each one give as he
purposes in his heart, not grudgingly or of necessity; for God
loves a cheerful giver.** And God is able to make all grace abound*

toward you, that you, always having all sufficiency in all things, have an abundance for every good work." (II Corinthians 9:6 8)

These powerful verses have been preached so often that many of us could quote them. They are of course, very true and dynamic principles, and Paul is doing some legitimate teaching to a church which has made commitments, but is a little sluggish in fulfilling them. He is using a little "personal advantage" motivation perhaps, but he does conclude with the statement that when they have everything they need, they will also have an abundance to give to the "good work," which of course is to expand the Kingdom of God.

A couple of chapters later Paul shares with the Corinthians the following:

"Did I commit sin in abasing myself that you might be exalted, **because I preached the gospel of God to you free of charge? I robbed other churches, taking wages from them to minister to you.** *And when I was present with you, and in need, I was a burden to no one, for what was lacking to me the brethren who came from Macedonia supplied. And in everything I kept myself from being burdensome to you, and so I will keep myself." (II Corinthians 11:7-9)*

Here is another of the many references where Paul declared that he would rather go without than ask for money. In this case, he declares that others supported him while he was serving them. When he declared, "I robbed other churches," he is really saying to them that they took from other churches, since they should have been supporting him themselves.

Galatians

In the book of Galatians we find some very relevant passages:

*"and when James, Cephas, and John, who seemed to be pillars, perceived the grace that had been given to me, they gave me and Barnabas the right hand of fellowship, that we should go to the Gentiles and they to the circumcised. **They desired only that we should remember the poor,** the very thing which I also was eager to do." (Galatians 2:9, 10)*

This passage again reveals the apostolic administration of finances as well as the clear fact that all the apostles were concerned that the needs of the poor were taken care of. Later Paul addresses the needs of those who minister:

"Let him that is taught the word share in all good things with him who teaches. *Do not be deceived, God is not mocked; for **whatever a man sows, that he will also reap.** For he who sows to his flesh will of the flesh reap corruption, but he who sows to the Spirit will of the Spirit reap everlasting life. And let us not grow weary while doing good, for in due season we shall reap if we do not lose heart. Therefore, as we have opportunity, **let us do good to all, especially to those who are of the household of faith."** (Galatians 6:6-10)*

This passage starts out focusing on the needs of those who teach, stating again that those who minister should live from the ministry. It also reminds the Galatians of the sowing and reaping principle. Then it exhorts them to do good whenever they can, especially to other believers.

Philippians

Paul says nothing relevant to this study in Ephesians, but concludes his epistle to the Philippians, one of the churches of Macedonia, with this wonderful passage:

*"But I rejoiced in the Lord greatly that now at last your care for me has flourished again; though you surely did care, but you lacked opportunity. Not that I speak in regard to need, **for I have learned in whatever state I am, to be content**; I know how to be abased, and I know how to abound. Everywhere and in all things I have learned both to be full and to be hungry, both to abound and to suffer need. **I can do all things through Christ who strengthens me**. Nevertheless you have done well that you shared in my distress.*

*Now you Philippians know also that in the beginning of the gospel, when I departed from Macedonia, no church shared with me concerning giving and receiving but you only. For even in Thessalonica you sent aid once and again for my necessities. **Not that I seek the gift, but I seek the fruit that abounds to your account.** Indeed I have all and abound. I am full, having received from Epaphroditus the things which were sent from you, a sweet-smelling aroma, an acceptable sacrifice, well pleasing to God. **And my God shall supply all your need according to His riches in glory by Christ Jesus.** (Philippians 4:10-19)*

This passage is quite self-explanatory, but it does confirm that Paul, as an apostle was willing to live in poverty as well as in prosperity if it would further the Kingdom of God.

I Thessalonians

Our next significant reference is in I Thessalonians:

"So affectionately longing for you, we were well pleased to impart to you not only the gospel of God, but also our own lives, because you had become dear to us. For you remember, brethren, our labor and toil; for laboring night and day, that we might not be a burden

to any of you, we preached to you the gospel of God." (I Thessalonians 2:8, 9)

Here we see that it wasn't just in Corinth that Paul worked with his hands to support himself. The Thessalonians, were recipients of many compliments from Paul, who loved them dearly, but it seems they were either unable or lacked the character or understanding to fully support Paul while he was with them.

II Thessalonians

Paul comes back to the support issue in his second epistle to the Thessalonians:

*"nor did we eat anyone's bread free of charge, but worked with labor and toil night and day, that we might not be a burden to any of you, not because we do not have authority, but to make ourselves an example of how you should follow us. Not because we do not have authority, but to make ourselves an example of how you should follow us. For even when we were with you, we commanded you this: **If anyone will not work, neither shall he eat.**" (II Thessalonians 3:8-10)*

Here Paul reinforces a strong work ethic at the same time as he repeats the fact that he has worked hard not to be a burden to them.

I Timothy

The next relevant passages are found in I Timothy. The first is in the third chapter in the context of the instructions for choosing deacons and bishops. The latter term probably is just a different descriptive word (meaning overseers), for leaders normally called elders, which we may also call pastors. A requirement for both offices

are that they be those who are **"not greedy for money."** This requirement is also repeated in Titus, where Paul talks about appointing
elders and then switches to the term, "bishops," apparently using
both terms to talk about the same person. (Titus 1:5-7)

Another passage in chapter five, deals with widows and their
support by the church. Paul makes it clear that only those who are
truly needy and at least 60 years old should receive regular support
from the church. It also makes clear that families should take care
of their own family members, and not expect the church to bear the
burden when it is their responsibility.

Finally we come to a very significant passage for our study:

"Let the elders who rule well be counted worthy of double
honor, especially those who labor in the word and doctrine.
For the Scripture says, 'You shall not muzzle an ox while it treads
out the grain,' and 'The laborer is worthy of his wages.'" (I Timo-
thy 5:17, 18)

Here is really the clearest Scripture that gives us instructions
regarding paying local church staff. The elders are the only ones
mentioned, but that doesn't mean that other local ministries were not
supported. Paul declares that the elders that rule well should be given
double honor. In the Greek the word rule means to preside over or
supervise. This, in the setting of the local church, is a function of the
elder, which we have equated with the term, "pastor." The "honor"
mentioned is a financial term, indicating wages, as is confirmed in
Paul's quote, "The laborer is worthy of his wages."

Thus local elders who administrate the local church and do it well
should be well paid. Notice also that the term "elders" is, as usual,
in the plural, rather than singular. It seems clear here, and in Acts
20, that there were multiple elders in every church. There is never a
mention of "the elder" or "pastor" or "head elder," etc. The reason is
that they didn't need a head elder, when there were apostles moving

among them providing the headship for them.

The next significant point here is that some, but not all elders labor (work hard to the point of weariness) in the word (logos) and doctrine (teaching). In other words, some elders (or pastors) have teaching gifts, but not all. This is another argument in favor of the idea that there are five different ministry gifts, rather than only four, the last being pastor/teacher. All elders supervise the flock, just like a shepherd, but not all are teachers. The ones who do it well, and also work hard to teach the Word of God, are worthy of extra wages.

Another possible interpretation of this passage is that the term elder could refer to the teacher as well as the pastor. Both of them could be called elders, which really means a senior or older person. The problem with this theory is that the local elders from Ephesus in Acts 20 were all called to be "shepherds" of the flock. As we discussed earlier, many teachers have little shepherding or "pastoral" gifts.

The third and probably most important point in our study is that **Paul, the senior apostle, was instructing the younger apostle, Timothy, to administrate the finances of the church. This indicates that it was the apostles who received and administrated the finances at this stage, rather than the elders.**

In chapter six Paul discusses the value of contentment again:

*" . . . men of corrupt minds and destitute of the truth, who suppose that godliness is a means of gain. From such withdraw yourself. But **godliness with contentment is great gain**. For we brought nothing into this world, and it is certain we can carry nothing out. And **having food and clothing, with these we shall be content**. But those who desire to be rich fall into temptation and a snare, and into many foolish and harmful lusts which drown men in destruction and perdition. For **the love of money is a root of all kinds of evil, for which some have strayed from the faith in their greediness and pierced themselves through with many sorrows**. But you, O man of God, flee these things and pursue*

102

righteousness, godliness, faith, love, patience, gentleness." (
I Timothy 6:5-11)

Again the teaching from the older apostle to the younger apostle is very clear. Not only leaders, but all who follow Christ should be aware of the dangers of seeking personal wealth for personal gain. Contentment is of great value. Greediness brings sorrow to ourselves and others. Perhaps apostles who teach about finances today should sound a little more like Paul, and give the balanced perspective that he brings to us.

Another verse later in the chapter gives the following exhortation to Timothy:

"Command those who are rich in this present age not to be haughty, nor to trust in uncertain riches but in the living God, who gives us richly all things to enjoy. **Let them do good, that they be rich in good works, ready to give, willing to share, storing up for themselves a good foundation for the time to come,** *that they may lay hold on eternal life." (I Timothy 6:17-19)*

Here again Paul the apostle is admonishing the junior apostle to be bold and to **command** the rich folk in the church not to think of themselves as better than others or to trust in their riches, but rather to be generous and share their blessings. These were exhortations that were not needed in the "Early Acts" church when unity and love produced powerful signs and wonders, which in turn produced incredible generosity. But these exhortations were needed when Paul wrote this letter and they are unfortunately still needed in most Christian circles today.

James

We find no more significant passages on finances until we come to the book of the apostle James, the half-brother of Jesus. In chapter two of this book, written to the twelve tribes who were scattered abroad, he warns the brethren not to sin by showing partiality to the rich. He exhorts them:

"Listen, my beloved brethren: Has God not chosen the poor of this world to be rich in faith and heirs of the kingdom which He promised to those who love Him? But you have dishonored the poor man. Do not the rich oppress you and drag you into the courts? Do they not blaspheme that noble name by which you are called?" (James 2:5-7)

James obviously sees a problem in the Jewish churches with leaders showing favoritism to the rich. Therefore, he is trying to show them the positive things about the poor and the negative things about the rich.

This passage has an indirect but still significant impact on our study. Obviously, the rich have the capacity to give more than the poor. Probably, finances were not overabundant in the church and the leaders were motivated by their financial need. Thus they slipped into the root sin of serving themselves, rather than serving Jesus, by showing favoritism.

This selfish, subtle and self-serving attitude comes into play without any premeditation. It is simply the nature of our flesh. James, an apostle, is correcting the way they allow money to control their behavior. This tendency to let finances dictate how we minister really comes into play today, especially for those ministries whose income depends on special offerings or donations.

Another point we need to make again is that we see the apostolic supervision of things related to finances in the church. James is responding to his apostolic responsibility to supervise the financial affairs of the churches in his apostolic sphere.

The next related passage comes a few verses later in a discussion of faith and works.

"If a brother or sister is naked and destitute of daily food, and one of you says to them, 'Depart in peace, be warmed and filled,' but you do not give them the things which are needed for the body, what does it profit?"

In this passage it is clear that **individual Christians are expected to do good works of charity and give to the needy, rather than waiting for the church to do it all.** James wants them to be like the "Early Acts" church, when people gave joyfully to everyone who had a need.

The final chapter of James begins with a rebuke to the rich who have lived in pleasure and luxury, while they robbed their laborers of their rightful wages. His attack is rather strong and scathing. This book is certainly not a prosperity preacher's primary source. But it is valuable in its warning that we should guard our motives in the church when it comes to finances.

I John

The only other passages in the New Testament epistles which are remotely related to our study are found in the epistles of John. The first, in I John 3:17, again declares that when we have this world's goods, we ought to meet a brother's needs, or we really don't have the love of God. In other words, individuals should be involved in direct charity, not depending on the church to do it all.

II John

The second passage which is very well known is in II John 2. It is a prayer that Gaius, a friend of John, would *"prosper in all things and be in health, just as your soul prospers."*

This is simply a statement about John's desire that his friend be blessed in every way, including material possessions. It certainly can be applied to each of us, since John clearly had the heart of God in all his inspired writings and what John wished for Gaius, God certainly wishes for us. It does tie in the natural blessings with the prosperity of the soul. It seems consistent with the principle that the closer we walk with God, the purer our motives will be and the more God can trust us with financial blessings.

This is the end of our search in the epistles for passages that relate to the collection and distribution of church finances. We will now try to come to some reasonable conclusions and applications from this study.

Summary and Interpretation of Biblical Financial Data

The first and most important truth we can emphatically declare from the biblical record is that **the real source of our problems with collecting and distributing finances is not how we administrate it, but rather the lack of enthusiasm and excitement in the church that makes people love to give.** We can make helpful adjustments in the way we administrate finances, but the root problem is the lack of unity, which produces the power, which produces the miracles, which produces excitement and enthusiasm and strong faith, both in the believer and in the unbeliever.

The source of unity, which leads to the other blessings, is brokenness and humility. The unity of the 120 in the upper room came after the apostles had all failed the Lord at the cross and then been forgiven. Their pride was crushed and having been forgiven much, they loved much. They became passionate to reveal that love and serve their Savior and Master. Their motives changed and the result was a pure administration of the power of the Holy Spirit through them as a team, rather than a collection of ego-driven superstars.

Having said this, we can see that part of the solution is to recognize the God-ordained leadership and administrative authority given to apostles. When true apostles, who have been with Jesus and have been sent to represent Him on the earth, are empowered to administrate His Kingdom, followers will be molded by their character and heart. The result will be greater humility, unity and power, which will produce greater joy, enthusiasm and hilarious giving.

We also need to listen to the burden of the Lord that comes through the prophets he has put in the church. The supernatural aspect of prophetic foreknowledge adds an element of excitement that helps people release their resources for the benefit of the Kingdom of God.

There is a place for teaching financial principles to motivate the saints to take part in the service of giving. And no one has more authority and influence than those who are recognized as apostles.

On the other hand, apostles should be willing to both teach and model personal sacrifice for the sake of the Kingdom of God. Paul willingly endured much suffering and imprisonment and preached and practiced contentment in whatever kind of circumstances he found himself.

Church leaders, including elders and deacons, should be free of greed, which is warned about many times in the epistles. Preferring the rich over the poor is also warned against by James, who had strong words against the rich who abused the poor among them.

Another very significant point for our study is that apostles were the administrators of the churches finances. They were either directly or indirectly involved in receiving and distributing funds and in teaching the principles of giving and receiving, and sowing and reaping.

The most important result of such a shift in responsibility to recognized apostles would be a shift in the distribution of finances. We would see more funds directed toward evangelistic outreaches. Many of these would be as a result of apostolic and prophetic strategy sessions, and would combine the resources of various local church and para-church ministries.

All five-fold ministries would be supported to some extent. Those who preach the Word should live from the ministry, according to Paul, and those who labor in the Word and teaching, should be worthy of double honor. Apostles who should have the most responsibility in the administration of finances, should not be hindered by lack of money from fulfilling their calling to care for those under their oversight. But clearly they should be willing to make personal sacrifices when necessary. Prophets, on the other hand, would often just as soon live by faith and not take a salary at all. Apostles should none-the-less see to it that their needs are not going unmet.

I am certainly not advocating an immediate radical upheaval in the methods of financing church ministries. The changes will probably take place gradually and only as apostles gain recognition and respect among the leadership of a broad spectrum of church and para-church ministries. Ultimately, I trust we will be able to totally replace the present system of financing para-church ministries through incessant appeals, which often bring shame to the name of Jesus. They would instead be financed with gifts from apostolic councils that deem their ministries worthy of support. Or better yet, the ministry of para-church ministries would be somehow absorbed into the "church of the city," a union of different churches of various cities.

The finances would originally come to the apostles from enthusiastic giving from both rich and poor, who are excited about the awesome miracles that are taking place. Tithing would not be a real issue. Christians would be giving sacrificially, which would far exceed their tithes. Many new converts who witness and experience supernatural healing and deliverance, will be among the most generous givers. **The secret, of course, is to empower the apostles and prophets to be what they are called to be so that they can empower the other ministries and initiate the exciting "happenings" that will catapult the church to a new level of glory.**

With all of this accumulated research information and analysis, let us now move on to visualizing the restored church of the twenty-first century, As we proceed we will try to suggest some positive steps in the right direction to take the church of Jesus Christ to its place of destiny in the twenty-first century.

Chapter 7

ENVISIONING THE FUTURE CHURCH IN ACTION

What will the church of the future look like, and how will we get there? We want to see the big picture with faith that "with God all things are possible."

Greater Recognition and Acceptance of Apostles and Prophets

I believe that God revealed something to me before the official change of the millennium, late in the year A.D. 2000. I saw God shaking up the old foundation and clearing the ground so that He could lay the true foundation of the apostles and prophets. I hadn't yet seen Dr. C. Peter Wagner's book entitled, *"Churchquake."* But quickly, I saw apostles and prophets from many different Christian movements coming together to develop relationships with each other and to listen to what God was speaking through the others.

Personally, God has asked me to move in this very direction, to help bring ministry leaders together in various regions, where God has given us favor. We are beginning to see a unity of heart and purpose in so many leaders, all of whom have a desire to see God's glory above their own personal ambitions.

This move of God will bring us to the place where very quickly the terms apostle and prophet will be as widely accepted as the terms, pastor, evangelist and teacher. With the acceptance of the terms will come an acceptance of their functions and roles in the ongoing progress of the church.

Most ministers we presently call "pastors" will instead be called apostles. But they will function much more like biblical apostles than they do today. That is, they will not just care for their own church ministry, but they will regularly meet with other apostles in the city, as well as with prophets who are committed to hearing from God on their behalf. Others will be regional, national or international apostles, administrating the Kingdom of God in their particular spheres of authority. See C. Peter Wagner's book, *"Spheres of Authority."*

We see this process beginning with leaders of various churches and movements. In Colorado Springs, Ted Haggard leads a church of several thousand, but he has become an apostle of the city. "Pastor" Haggard has shared his heart with the "pastors" of the city, and in many cases has sent resources from his own congregation to other churches in the time of their need. Even pastors, who opposed him out of jealousy and fear of losing their members, became friends after receiving significant aid from Ted Haggard's congregation.[2]

Another step in the right direction was reported to us by a senior apostolic "pastor" in Canada. He reported that another large church in his city was actually given large donations from at least two other downtown churches of different denominations, those who could have been considered competition in their area. One of the churches gave $100,000.00 for their building fund. We minister in this Canadian city several weeks of every year. Over the last few years we have seen an incredible openness among the city's spiritual leaders to the concept of seeking God together and praying with and for one another. Signs of revival are clearly taking place in that city.

The same leader, who gave us the above information, also was recently acknowledged by his own church leadership as an apostle of their church. His church is in a denomination with a typical church government composed of a local board, which has always hired and fired their pastors. The church went through a major structural change, choosing to transition to a five-fold ministry form of government. Although there was some resistance, the transition has taken place and the church is learning to adjust to a different infrastructure. Now this apostolic leader is considering putting other ministries, such as prophets and evangelists, on church salary, with the freedom to minister outside the church for much of the year.

Other Five-Fold Ministries Find Their Niche

As apostles and prophets begin to function more and more in their true roles, they will work together to release the other ministries to fulfill their destinies. These ministries will be more effective and anointed than ever before, because they will not be asked to spend time doing as many things that they are not gifted for. The true pastors and teachers won't be asked to administrate things they have no interest in, nor will they be expected to do all the work of the evangelist. Instead evangelists will be encouraged and sometimes financed to bring in the lost.

The results of the work of the evangelists will bring excitement to the pastors and teachers, who love to nourish and teach the excited new converts. Most of us have witnessed what even one new and excited convert can do for the morale of the church. When they are coming in every week or every day, the excitement will really accelerate.

As discussed earlier, the apostles and prophets will involve themselves with the new converts and begin to bring some guidance to help them develop their God-given gifts to fulfill their destiny. Soon many of them will be mentored by leaders with similar gifts and they will be on their way to becoming leaders themselves and willing soldiers on the front lines for God. Many will become evangelists. Some of these will later transition into other ministries, but they will always have a love for lost souls.

Powerful Revivals Will Break Out

Certain cities or regions will become the target of concentrated intercessory prayer and evangelism, as directed by the Holy Spirit through the apostles and prophets. Local leaders will find themselves working together for the good of the Kingdom of God, rather than just for their own ministry. Leaders and evangelists from other regions will be sent by God to fan the flames, and tremendous moves of God will occur. The critics of Holy Spirit revivals will have their hands full, because they will be springing up in many places in rapid succession.

Toronto and Pensacola, Florida, were forerunners of the power that will be released in the next few years. The prophetic signs and wonders, such as falling, shaking, gold fillings, etc. of the past decades, will be superceded by the more practical signs and wonders. These will include a multitude of creative miracles, supernatural provision, divine transportation (as in Philip's ministry), and many other demonstrations of God's power, such as raising the dead. All of these have begun to increase, not only in Third World Countries, but in North America as well.

The results will be spontaneous crusades and street evangelism, with thousands coming to Christ in a short period of time. Regions of the world which have already experienced revival will be assisted in administrating the revival and bringing their people and their various movements into a powerful unity.

The flames of revival will be carried to every city and town, with powerful results. Apostles and prophets will receive an increase in their anointing and rise to the occasion to provide the leadership needed to administrate and sustain this great explosion of new growth in the church. Other ministries will also receive new grace and power to help disciple the converts.

Walls of Division Will Crumble

The major divisions in the body of Christ will almost disappear. Both those in the Pentecostal/- Charismatic camp and those in the Evangelical/- Fundamentalist camp will be convicted of spiritual pride and lack of love for the rest of the body of Christ. The minor divisions will also be eliminated. Baptists will make peace with other Baptists. Pentecostals of various brands will develop strong relationships with other Pentecostals.

In April, 2002, a meeting called "Together 2002" was held in Washington, D. C. It marked the first time that "top leaders from all the streams of Pentecost—classical, charismatic, Oneness, Word of Faith, Third Wave— came together in a spirit of unity, not to discuss doctrinal differences, but to rejoice in their common spiritual heritage."[3] This meeting was a follow-up to a 50-hour prayer vigil held in Atlanta, Georgia, in 2001, and attended by thousands of Pentecostal leaders and lay members. These gatherings are just forerunners of greater things to come.

What will break down these long-standing walls of division? The greatest weapon against division is Holy Spirit empowered love. I have seen this in action while in Argentina in 1973. When the first miracles began to happen in the city of Cordoba, joy and love became extremely tangible and local pastors quickly reconciled to each other, asking forgiveness for various things. **No one wanted to be left out when God was moving, and differences seemed so petty when Jesus, Himself, showed up through His special gifts and ministries.** (See Psalm 68:18)

As the apostles and prophets humbly lead the church into revival, those who have not believed in the supernatural will be faced with the reality of God's power in many ways. In many cases, these people, including leaders, will find themselves desperately in need of a miracle. They will not be able to resist asking for prayer from those who are flowing with the revival. Others will just be overcome by the spirit of grace and love that is extended to them by people who have been touched by the revival. I predict that a large number of powerful leaders and churches will have major shake-ups in their doctrine and experience. I expect this to touch some of the leading evangelical, fundamentalist and seeker-friendly churches, as well as those in Pentecostal and charismatic circles.

Prayer Power and Radical Faith Will Invade Hostile Nations

As world-wide revival gains momentum, many passionate Christians will hear the cry of at least two billion souls living in nations very hostile to Christianity. These include the nations still embracing communism, such as China, as well as the entire Muslim world. I believe that radical Christians, who have been transformed by Jesus, and have an overpowering love for Him will find themselves in deep travail for the souls held in these prisons of spiritual darkness.

The results of this powerful intercession will be that many cracks will be found in the bamboo curtain and in Muslim resistance to Christianity. Three major things will take place to enable the gospel to invade these nations.

1. First of all, God will respond to the intercession with personal visitations to people behind these national prison walls. Already we have heard of many Muslims, who have become believers in Jesus after having visions and dreams and angelic visitations. George Otis Jr. reported recently at an Illinois conference, that in one of the Muslim nations, formerly a part of the Soviet Union, it has become a wonderful epidemic. Large numbers of Muslims have become Christians because of divine supernatural appearances in their nation.

2. The second phenomenon will be that many sold-out and radical Christians will be willing to lay down their lives and find ways into these countries to evangelize the lost. Some will indeed make

the supreme sacrifice, but none of their lives will be given in vain. Revivals will break out in unexpected places and a great harvest of souls will take place.

3. The third means God will use will be the shaking up of the political leadership in many of these nations, which will bring a new level of freedom to the citizens. Some of these nations will be radically changed from the top down. Then great armies of believers will invade and follow the earlier trailblazers, many of whom will have paid the price of their own blood shed for the gospel of Jesus Christ. The combined result of the above events will be a tremendous harvest of souls for the Kingdom of God.

Satanic Opposition Will Intensify Against Church and Revival

As the revival described in the previous pages progresses, the enemy will become more and more furious and will use those whom he has possessed with all the evil power he can muster. This will manifest in many false accusations and persecutions such as Nero made against the Christians in the early church. Great spiritual warfare will take place in preparation for the final events of this age and the return of Jesus to this earth.

At this point we will abstain from making further predictions and how this all fits in with any particular view of eschatology. The obvious conclusion however, is that when the final harvest is taking place, there will be a separation of the wheat from the tares and then the Lord of the harvest will receive the harvest unto Himself. But the gospel will be preached in every nation and the whole world will know who Jesus is.

Final Conclusions

The apostolic and prophetic reformation is now in full swing. It is not just a "new thing" or a spiritual fad. The restoration of the apostles and prophets into their proper places in the foundation of the church, and into their proper functions in the body of Christ will bring about a powerful release of all five special gift-ministries. This will restore the church of Jesus to its most powerful condition since the "Early Acts" church. And before the return of Jesus "the glory of the latter house will exceed the glory of the former house." (Haggai 2:9)

To accomplish this, God has authorized a major shaking of the old foundations, with the result that many old traditions and methods are being replaced by the unfamiliar, but more biblical, ways and means. Those who love their religious traditions more than they love God and His Kingdom will find it very difficult to release the old to make room for the new. But God's plan will prevail and His people must make the necessary adjustments.

For most people the benefits of the new will far outweigh the loss of the old, and great excitement will begin to attract the unbelievers. Curiosity and hunger for reality will draw people to the "new thing" that's happening among the believers. All five ministries will spring into action to win and disciple the seekers. The whole body of Jesus will be activated to play a role in the explosive expansion of the Kingdom of God world-wide.

Apostles will be in unity with other apostles and prophets. Some will be more "on stage" than others, but all will have their input into administrative decisions. Evangelists will be reaping the fruit hand over fist and pastors and teachers will have so many "eager beaver" converts, that they will be almost overwhelmed.

I firmly believe that all of the above will take place in various parts of the world at various rates of progress. In the end, people in every nation will hear the gospel and be brought into the Kingdom of God.

So if you find yourself being pushed out of your comfort zone of relative obscurity and into the middle of an interactive group of believers, be assured that God wants to use your gifts to help someone else in the group, while He blesses you through the others' gifts at the same time. So get ready to join the football huddle (Chapter

1) and dedicate the gifts that God has given you to benefit the team. In allowing yourself to become a part of the team, and giving your all to the Kingdom of God, you will find incredible fulfillment and freedom to be all that God intended you to be.

If you remain open to change in things that have always been the same, and if you allow God to remove the foundation that you have always had under your feet, get ready to become part of His beautiful and gloriously restored house. It's a house where God's presence is as real as the crystal chandelier hanging from the gold-plated rafters.

It's a house where everyone feels totally safe, supremely loved and truly needed. It's a house where there is no shortage of delicious food or provision for every need. It's the house of your dreams. But more importantly, it's the house of His dreams. Let's be willing to let Him do what He needs to do to build His house?

Jesus is the master builder, and He makes no mistakes. Let Him finish what He has begun. He is restoring the original foundation, and the rest of the beautiful building will quickly follow, complete with walls and roof, doors and windows. Solomon's temple will totally pale in comparison and once again the Glory of the Lord will fill His temple.

Even so Lord Jesus, build Your temple. Use us in every way You can. Do what You must to help us fit smoothly next to the other stones in the building. We look forward to being a part of Your finished product—a temple for Your glory. Amen!

RECOMMENDED READING LIST

Cannistraci, David. *The Gift of Apostle,* Ventura, CA: Regal, 1996
—*Apostles and the Emerging Apostolic Movement,* Ventura, CA: Regal, 2000

Deere, Jack. *Beginners Guide to the Gift of Prophecy,* Ann Arbor, MI: Servant Publications, 2001.

Gentile, Earnest B. *Your Sons and Daughters Shall Prophesy,* Grand Rapids, MI: Chosen Books, 2001.

Hamon, Dr. Bill. *Prophets and Personal Prophecy,* Shippensburg, PA: Destiny Image Publishers, Inc., 1987.
—*Prophets and the Prophetic Movement,* Shippensburg, PA: Destiny Image, 1990.
—*Prophets: Pitfalls and Principles,* Shippensburg, PA: Destiny Image, 1991.
—*Apostles, Prophets and the Coming Moves of God ,* Shippensburg, PA: Destiny Image, 1997.
—*The Day of The Saints,* Shippensburg, PA: Destiny Image, 2002.

Jacobs, Cindy. *The Voice of God,* Ventura, CA: Regal, 1995.

Joyner, Rick. *The Final Quest,* New Kensington, PA: Whitaker House, 1997.
—*The Call,* New Kensington, PA: Whitaker House, 2000.
—*Prophetic Vision For the Twenty-First Century,* Nashville, TN: Nelson/W Publishing Group, 1999.

Maxwell, John. *Failing Forward,* Nashville, TN: Nelson/W Publishing Group, 2000.

Peters, Ben R. *The Dynamics of Biblical Prophetic Ministry,* Elgin, IL: Victory Litho, 2001. Available from Open Heart Ministries (www. ohmint.org).

—*Heal Your Body Lord,* Elgin, IL: Victory Litho, 2001. (www.ohmint. org).

—*Signs and Wonders—To Seek or Not to Seek,* Fairfax, VA: Xulon Press, 2002

Randolph, Larry. *User Friendly Prophecy,* Century City, CA: Cherith, 1995.

Sanford, John and Paula. *The Elijah Task,* Tulsa, OK: Victory House, Inc. 1977.

Sanford, John. *Elijah Among Us,* Grand Rapids, MI: Chosen Books, 2002.

Silvoso, Ed. *Anointed For Business,* Ventura, CA: Regal, 2002

Wagner, Dr. C. Peter. *Apostles and Prophets,* Ventura, CA: Regal, 2000.

—*Churchquake,* Ventura, CA: Regal 1999.

—*The New Apostolic Churches,* Ventura, CA: Regal, 1998.

—*Spheres of Authority,* Colorado Springs, CO: Wagner Publications, 2002.

—Your Spiritual Gifts Can Help Your Church Grow, Ventura, CA: Regal, 2000.

ENDNOTES

[1] C. Peter Wagner, *Apostles and Prophets* (Ventura CA: Regal Books, 2000) p. 5.

[2] Ted Haggard, *Primary Purpose* (Orlando, Florida: Creation House, 1995)

[3] August 2002, Volume 28, Number 1, Charisma & Christian Life Magazine, p. 20

Ben R. Peters

With over 40 years of ministry experience, Ben Peters with his wife, Brenda, have been called to an international apostolic ministry of equipping and activating others with a passion for sending laborers into the harvest fields of the earth, including the seven mountains of society. As founders and directors first of Open Heart Ministries, and now the Kingdom Sending Center, Ben and Brenda have ministered to tens of thousands with teaching and prophetic ministry. The result is that many have been saved, healed, delivered and activated into powerful ministries of their own.

Ben has been given significant insights for the body of Christ and has written sixteen books in the past ten years, since beginning a full-time itinerant ministry. His passions and insights include unity in the body of Christ, accessing the glory of God, five-fold team ministry, prophetic ministry, and signs and wonders for the world-wide harvest.

Kingdom Sending Center
P.O. Box 25
Genoa, IL 60135

www.KingdomSendingCenter.org
ben.peters@kingdomsendingcenter.org

Made in the USA
San Bernardino, CA
13 November 2013